To

Mum

With Love

Janet

XOXOX

G000093472

Paths *of* Peace

Paths *of* Peace

*A weekly devotional walk
with God through the year*

Beryl Adamsbaum

FOREWORD BY
Jennifer Rees Larcombe

Blessed is the man who finds wisdom … Her ways are pleasant ways, and all her paths are peace.

Proverbs 3:13,17

Acknowledgements

Many people have accompanied me on my walk with the Lord at different stages of my life and have, therefore, without knowing it, contributed in some way to this collection of poems and devotionals. It would be impossible to mention them all by name.

No doubt more people than I could imagine have prayed for me over the years, beginning, I am sure, with my grandparents. As a child in Zambia, I came to know the Lord thanks to a missionary family. Later, as a student in Liverpool, I was nurtured through an inter-varsity group, one former member of which kindly read through an early draft of my manuscript. I thank Bruce Millar for his helpful comments, suggestions and corrections. My teachers at the Bible School in Paris that I attended with my husband Derek were also instrumental in my spiritual growth. Pastors and members of the churches we have served in Geneva have had precious input as well. To all these people I am deeply grateful, including Cathy Mc Nerney who also reviewed the manuscript for me.

And the Lord has been with me through it all, inspiring and equipping me. He has encouraged me in times of difficulty and enabled me to persevere. I trust that the result will bring glory to Him.

Contents

Autumn

Winter

Foreword

This is a truly beautiful book! It has lived beside my bed for the
last few weeks and I've savoured it in small instalments, with my
morning cup of tea. It makes me feel as if someone has poured cool,
clean water right through my soul and spirit, leaving me nourished and
refreshed.

Of course, the book is not supposed to be read in just a few weeks; it
ought to have stayed by my bed for a whole year, so that it could link the
changing seasons with the varying scenery of my spiritual journey: the
happy peacefulness of summer, the busy fruitfulness of autumn, the wintry
'dark night of the soul' and the glorious reawakening of springtime. So I
shall just have to give myself the pleasure of reading it all over again more
slowly.

In the past I have often been blessed by Beryl's Bible reading notes.
Her deep knowledge and love of the Bible is catching; but this book is not
just a Bible reading system – it is far more than that. Beryl uses words as a
gifted artist uses brushes and shades of colour; and her use of poetry and
old hymns gives the book depth and grace. Yet her way of using anecdotes
from her everyday life, stories about ordinary people and memories of walks
in the countryside all combine to give an earthy relevance to her biblical
themes. While remaining firmly based in the real world it has the unusual
quality of lifting us above the endless string of little jobs that make up our
daily lives on planet Earth.

In Week 17 Beryl describes how she was hit by an attack of 'writer's
block' while working on *Paths of Peace*. Her mind went blank, all
inspiration died and she was on the point of giving up completely. As a

writer I heartily sympathise; and Beryl did exactly what I have often done in the same situation. She went out and walked with the Lord, pouring out to Him all her frustration. As she tramped along she felt He was reminding her of a passage in Exodus which she had recently been reading. It talks about the skilled craftsmen who were chosen to create the tabernacle and all its intricate furnishings (Exod. 35:30–33). They were not only gifted but also full of the Spirit of God. This is how Beryl describes what happened next; 'It was as if God were saying to me, "I want you to use the skills I have given you to produce something beautiful for Me ..." You are indwelt by My Spirit. Let Him inspire you.' Filled with new enthusiasm Beryl could hardly wait to get home and start working on the book once again. That explains for me why this book is so special; it is so obviously inspired by the Holy Spirit and it is indeed a thing of great beauty that will become a constant companion for many who walk in Beryl's footprints along the *Paths of Peace*.

Jennifer Rees Larcombe

Preface

I n this little volume entitled *Paths of Peace*, we attempt to walk with
God every day of each week, thanks to the meditations, Bible verses,
poems and prayers that will encourage us and accompany us on our
way. 'Walk in all the ways I command you,' says God, 'that it may go well
with you' (Jer. 7:23). The meditations and my own poems are of course
based on my own experience or on my understanding of God's Word, and
span fifty years, from the middle of the twentieth century into the twenty-
first. Alongside these I have quoted from older hymns and poems reflecting
similar thoughts and feelings expressed in ages past.

In Genesis chapter 2 we read, 'By the seventh day God had finished the
work he had been doing; so on the seventh day he rested from all his work'
(v.2). Divided into fifty-two meditations, inspired by God's rhythm in
creation, this book contains enough material to enable thoughtful but busy
people to engage in serious, leisurely reflection on each week's theme in
moments of peace and quiet gleaned from each day.

The fifty-two weeks of the year are divided into the four seasons, with
a short introduction to each season's walks. The themes are clearly stated
so as to enable the reader to dip into sections relevant to his or her current
preoccupations or needs. Many of the themes overlap. It is impossible to
talk about love for God without talking about obedience, for example.
Jesus said, 'If you love me, you will obey what I command' (John 14:15).
Similarly, the themes of endurance and perseverance have much in
common. Hope, love, joy, peace and faith are mentioned in several parts of
the book. The meditation about our journey through life contains thoughts

that recur in 'Walking purposefully' and 'Walking towards the goal'.

And this is how it should be, for the Christian life cannot be compartmentalised. It forms a whole. If I am a follower of Jesus, then I will live for Him and try to please Him wherever I am and whatever I may be doing. I will walk with Him at home and at work and during my leisure moments.

Our journey through life is not always easy. We often face temptations, trials, maybe even tragedy. Walking with God can transform life's situations, bringing peace amid the pain, light in the darkness of our suffering and hope in times of despair. God will direct our steps: '… your ears will hear a voice behind you, saying, "This is the way; walk in it"' (Isa. 30:21). As you walk along God's paths, through the seasons of each year, open your eyes to the beauty around you. See God's hand in all that He has made. Draw close to Him and learn of Him.

I trust that the poems, prayers and meditations in this little book will make you more aware of the Lord's presence, and that through them you will be encouraged to walk with God each day. May God draw close to you and bless you as you walk in His 'pleasant ways', in 'paths [of] peace'.

Spring

'Nothing is so beautiful as spring', wrote Gerard Manley Hopkins. I am inclined to agree! New life in plants and animals evokes a joyful response in me. In early spring, in France where I live, yellow is the preponderant colour – forsythia, primroses, daffodils, then laburnum and rapeseed – all reflecting the sun's glory. On my walks I discover crocuses pushing their way up through the earth. Birds fill the air with music. Could the Garden of Eden have been more beautiful? 'Now the Lord God had planted a garden in the east, in Eden … And the Lord God made all kinds of trees grow out of the ground – trees that were pleasing to the eye and good for food' (Gen. 2:8–9).

Eating lunch at a lakeside restaurant, a friend and I spotted a majestic white swan with three young grey cygnets, two of which climbed onto the back of the mother, who lifted her wings to cover and protect them. What a picture of the peace and security we have in Christ! Jesus exclaims to the inhabitants of Jerusalem how much he longed to gather them 'as a hen gathers her chicks under her wings' (Matt. 23:37).

Next to an old château above Lake Geneva is an iris garden. The unique varieties and variegated colours of these flowers attract people from all over the world. God specialises in beauty and variety. He made us all different, and he wants to be in relationship with each one of us and walk with us each day in paths of peace.

Heaven above is softer blue, Earth around is sweeter green;
Something lives in every hue Christless eyes have never seen:
Birds with gladder songs o'erflow, Flowers with deeper beauties shine,
Since I know, as now I know, I am his, and he is mine.
George Wade Robinson, 1838–1877

Walking each day

… inwardly we are being renewed day by day.
2 Corinthians 4:16b

I enjoy walking. I try to get out and walk every day. Each season has its own beauty, from the brightly coloured flowers in spring to the shady trees in summer, with their ripening fruit. Then the autumn hues, and finally, in winter, the snow-capped mountains etched against a clear blue sky.

It's not quite so much fun to walk when it's raining! But we certainly need the rain. In the quiet and peace of the early morning, I am conscious of God's presence. Spending time with Him each day is a privilege and a blessing.

When the walls of Jerusalem had been rebuilt after the return from the Exile, Ezra the priest and scribe, read God's Word to the people every day. We read: 'Day after day, from the first day to the last, Ezra read from the Book of the Law of God' (Neh. 8:18a). That is because God's people need to spend time with Him each day, communing with Him in prayer, walking with Him, and feeding on His Word.

This daily renewal is a principle reiterated right throughout Scripture, beginning with the wilderness wanderings of the Israelites, recorded for us in the book of Exodus, where we first read of their complaints at having left behind in Egypt the food that they wanted. In response, God said to Moses, 'I will rain down bread from heaven for you. The people are to go out each day and gather enough for that day' (Exod. 16:4a). This bread, called 'manna' was to be collected daily. It could not be stored up. God provided for them afresh each day.

Similarly, each Christian needs to feed on God's Word daily. Jesus taught us to pray: 'Give us each day our daily bread' (Luke 11:3). Last year or last month, last week or even yesterday is not enough. Today is what counts. And the nourishment we receive today is for today. Tomorrow we must feed again. Likewise, Jesus tells us that if we are serious about wanting to follow Him we must take up our cross daily (Luke 9:23).

To know that we can come to Him day by day and ask Him to provide for us does away with a lot of stress and anxiety. Probably we have all been subject to fear at one time or another because of the uncertainty of life. 'Do not worry,' says Jesus in that beautiful passage in Matthew's Gospel (6:25–34), where He reminds us that if God feeds the birds, He will surely feed us, and if He 'clothes the grass of the field', then He will make sure that we have something to wear.

But we should not make these material needs our focus. Rather, we are to 'seek first his kingdom and his righteousness, and all these things will be given to [us] as well' (Matt. 6:33). Jesus tells His followers to live one day at a time: '… do not worry about tomorrow … Each day has enough trouble of its own' (Matt. 6:34).

Let us learn to live each day to the full, wholly committed to Christ, walking with Him, trusting Him, drawing our strength from Him, rejoicing in Him. Remember, 'This is the day the LORD has made; let us rejoice and be glad in it' (Psa. 118:24).

[His compassions] are new every morning
Lamentations 3:23a

Thank You, Lord, for the tremendous privilege of being able to come to
    You each day,
for daily renewal,
for daily provision.
Lord, each day, I want to draw close to You.

Each day I want to be conscious of Your presence.
Each day I want to know Your strength, Your wisdom, Your enabling,
   Your direction.
Each day I want to reflect Jesus Christ.
Each day I want to feed on Your Word.
Each day I want to be an instrument in Your hands and a channel of
   Your love.
Each day I want to walk with You.
Take my days, Lord.
Fill them with the light and love of Your presence.
May they count for eternity.

Day by day the manna fell;
Oh to learn this lesson well!
Still by constant mercy fed,
Give us, Lord, our daily bread.

'Day by day', the promise reads,
Daily strength for daily needs;
Cast foreboding fear away,
Take the manna of today.

Thou our daily task shalt give;
Day by day to Thee we live:
So shall added years fulfil
Not our own, our Father's will.

Josiah Conder
1852–1920

Day by day, dear Lord,
Of three things I pray:
To see Thee more clearly,
To love Thee more dearly,
To follow Thee more nearly
Day by day.

Richard of Chichester

1197–1253

Personal Reflections

Walking in fullness of joy

... in thy presence there is fullness of joy ...
Psalm 16:11, RSV

Sometimes we talk about being 'overjoyed'. What exactly is 'fullness of joy'? Do we have varying capacities for joy? If so, can our capacity grow? Yes, I think it can, through walking with God each day, and through gaining a deeper understanding of Him and of all that He has given us in Jesus – the joy of sins forgiven and new life.

Don't you feel a throb of joy when you begin to fathom a precious truth in the Bible that you did not understand before, or when you suddenly come across a part of Scripture that is relevant to your own particular situation or that can be perceived as an answer to your prayers?

Our capacity for joy can grow too as we gain a greater awareness of all that God has created. How many times have you experienced a thrill of joy when spotting a breathtaking view or panorama, or perceiving something else in nature: a flower, a tree covered in blossom, a leaf, a kitten or puppy, a rainbow, an intricately woven spider's web?

The following is an extract from my journal, dated 7 March 2000:

> As I walked to the prayer meeting this afternoon, I was conscious of deep joy welling up inside me as the sights and sounds of the spring day – brightly-coloured crocuses and the birdsong – caused me to praise the Lord for the beauty of his creation. Amid the joy, and in contrast to it, an ache and a deep longing became apparent within me. Is there such a thing as 'pure joy', I wonder? Maybe joy is always tinged with sadness, ephemeral and fleeting as it is, like the spring

flowers that inspired it. '… the wind blows over it and it is gone' (Psalm 103:16). But one day our 'joy will be complete' (John 15:11).

What about the joy of relationship – the joy of being in love; the joy of becoming a parent; the joy of friendship? The joy is real and can go very deep … but it is often mingled with pain. The Bible tells us that Jesus '… for the joy set before him endured the cross, scorning its shame …' (Heb. 12:2). There is joy beyond the pain. 'Weeping may tarry for the night, but joy comes with the morning' (Psa. 30:5b, RSV).

'I have told you this,' says Jesus to His disciples, 'so that my joy may be in you and that your joy may be complete' (John 15:11). What is Jesus referring to? What has He told them? He has been talking to them about love and obedience. In the previous verse He says, 'If you obey my commands, you will remain in my love …' In what way is our joy 'complete'? Our joy will be complete when we love and obey the Lord. That is something that we must aim for, even though we will never do it perfectly in this life. In comparison to God's love for me, my love for Him is weak and imperfect. But I show my love for Him through obeying Him. He says, 'If you love me, you will obey what I command' (John 14:15) and 'If anyone loves me, he will obey my teaching' (John 14:23).

The apostle Paul says that God '… richly provides us with everything for our enjoyment' (1 Tim. 6:17). So, let us enjoy all that God has given us. Let us walk in fullness of joy.

In all my prayers for all of you, I always pray with joy because of
your partnership in the gospel from the first day until now, being
confident of this, that he who began a good work in you will carry it
on to completion until the day of Christ Jesus.
Philippians 1:4–6

Thank You, Lord, for the joy of sins forgiven, for the joy of knowing You, and for the joy of close relationships. Help me to love You and to obey You so that my joy will be complete. Thank You for the joy that is set before us, which enables us to endure pain. Thank You for giving us all things richly to enjoy.

The prophet Isaiah, in beautiful poetry, writes of the joy of the redeemed:

> *The wilderness and the dry land shall be glad,*
> *the desert shall rejoice and blossom;*
> *like the crocus it shall blossom abundantly,*
> *and rejoice with joy and singing …*
> *then the lame shall leap like a deer,*
> *and the tongue of the speechless sing for joy …*
> *And the ransomed of the LORD shall return,*
> *and come to Zion with singing;*
> *everlasting joy shall be upon their heads;*
> *they shall obtain joy and gladness,*
> *and sorrow and sighing shall flee away.*
> Isaiah 35:1–2a,6,10, NRSV

'I bring you good news of great joy,' said the angel to the shepherds on the occasion of the birth of Jesus Christ (Luke 2:10). This announcement inspired Isaac Watts' hymn:

> *Joy to the world, the Lord has come!*
> *Let earth receive her King;*
> *Let every heart prepare him room*
> *And heaven and nature sing,*
> *And heaven and nature sing,*
> *and heaven, and heaven and nature sing!*

Joy to the earth, the Saviour reigns!
Your sweetest songs employ
While fields and streams and hills and plains
Repeat the sounding joy,
Repeat the sounding joy,
Repeat, repeat the sounding joy.

Isaac Watts

1674–1748

Personal Reflections

Walking in paths of peace

… the God of peace will be with you.
Philippians 4:9

'Peace on earth' seems rather an elusive commodity, to say the least. We only have to watch the news to see fighting in many parts of the world. Envy, greed, hatred, desire for revenge, make for a world where peace is at best precarious.

But surely things are different in our churches? Alas, how sad it is that we hear of splits and divisions within the Church. Let us determine, in so far as it depends on us, to 'Make every effort to live in peace with all men …' (Heb. 12:14).

But God. What hope and encouragement is contained in this little expression! It encourages us because it reminds us that God is sovereign and all-powerful. He is actively at work in circumstances beyond our control. He can transform situations. Even more wonderful, He can transform *us* and give us peace in times of adversity.

It is an expression found many times in the Scriptures. To quote just a few instances, let us look at some of the psalms. In Psalm 31, a psalm of David, the psalmist is in distress, weak with sorrow and grief, consumed by anguish, in fear of his life (vv.9–13). And yet he can say, '*But* I trust in you, O LORD' (v.14, my italics), and even though his circumstances have not changed by the end of the psalm, his focus has. Instead of focusing on his enemies, his eyes are on God, and the psalm ends on a peaceful note of hope and praise.

Psalm 102:12 is a cry of hope from one who, in intense suffering, can look up and exclaim, '*But* you, O LORD …' (my italics). This upward glance changes his perspective and enables him to live in peace, with the absolute assurance that God will intervene in some way. In each of these examples, the peace and assurance came *before* the situation actually changed. As soon as the psalmist looked away from his troubles and focused on God, he was comforted.

This peace is something we can all experience, for has not Jesus promised us rest if we come to Him? He says, 'Come to me, all you who are weary and burdened, and I will give you rest. Take my yoke upon you and learn from me, for I am gentle and humble in heart, and you will find rest for your souls. For my yoke is easy and my burden is light' (Matt. 11:28–30).

Paul promises freedom from anxiety and '... the peace of God, which transcends all understanding ...' (Phil. 4:7) if we bring our requests to God in '... prayer and supplication with thanksgiving ...' (Phil. 4:6, RSV).

Let us take the Lord at His word! Let us take our eyes off our circumstances and focus on Him who has promised us His rest and peace even in the midst of suffering. He says, 'Peace I leave with you; my peace I give you. I do not give to you as the world gives. Do not let your hearts be troubled and do not be afraid' (John 14:27).

He walked with me in peace and uprightness ...
Malachi 2:6b

Lord, make me an instrument of Thy peace.
Where there is hatred, let me sow love;
Where there is injury, let me sow pardon;
Where there is doubt, faith;
Where there is despair, hope;
Where there is darkness, light;
Where there is sadness, joy.

St Francis of Assisi
1182–1226

Paths of peace

Body wracked with pain
Tortured, crying out in agony.
And you talk of peace?

Loved one gone away,
Departed from this life forever.
And you talk of peace?

Relationship rent,
Broken. Friend cruel, faithless, untrue.
And you talk of peace?

Jesus suffered pain,
The agony of rejection too,
But rose victorious.

Over sin and death
He conquered. His victory is mine.
So I talk of peace.

Yes, the peace of God –
Peace which transcends all understanding –
Guards my heart and mind.

Personal Reflections

Walking with Jesus

As ye have therefore received Christ Jesus the Lord,
so walk ye in him.
Colossians 2:6, AV

My brother David loves to walk. His daughter Debbie gave him a dog. He writes:

> I walk miles with Mishka, minimum five miles a day, weather permitting. After all the years of living in Thornbury [south-west England], I've found some lovely walks through fields and woods that I never knew about. We meet lots of like-minded people. So we're both making new friends.

As I think of David and his dog on their walks, and the new friends they are making, my mind goes back to those two other friends, disciples of Jesus, walking along the road to Emmaus, with sad faces and sorrowful hearts. They were grieving. We read: 'They were talking with each other about everything that had happened' (Luke 24:14).

They were joined by a third person, who '... walked along with them' (Luke 24:15) and asked them what they were talking about. We read that 'They stood still, their faces downcast' (v.17b). Of course, we know who the other Person was, but these two people 'were kept from recognising him' (v.16) until Jesus later revealed Himself to them as He broke bread at the table that evening (vv.30–31).

The disciples had been slow to understand all that Jesus had taught them. They explained to their companion that they had hoped that Jesus of Nazareth '… was the one who was going to redeem Israel' (v.21a), but now He was dead and all hope was gone.

It occurred to me how privileged they were to be walking along the road in the company of the Son of God Himself! He actually drew alongside them and accompanied them on their way. He noticed their sadness and, in answer to His question, they told Him that Jesus of Nazareth had been crucified. In spite of already having been indirectly informed that Jesus was alive again, they obviously didn't really think that such a thing could be true. And here they were in the company of the risen Christ Himself!

Are we any less privileged? This same Jesus, risen from the dead, and ascended to the Father's right hand, has promised never to leave His children. He wants to walk along with us, just as He did with those two people on the road to Emmaus all those years ago.

Walking with Jesus implies being in relationship with Him, loving Him, dialoguing with Him, trusting Him, obeying Him. It means communing with Him, being close to Him, opening ourselves up to Him, sharing our concerns with Him. And it involves listening to Him, living in a way that is pleasing to Him, being in harmony with Him. Is He your daily companion? Are you walking with Jesus?

Whoever claims to live in him must walk as Jesus did.
1 John 2:6

O walk with Jesus, wouldst thou know
How deep, how wide his love can flow!
They only fail his love to prove
Who in the ways of sinners rove.

Walk thou with him; that way is light,
All other pathways end in night:
Walk thou with him; that way is rest;
All other pathways are unblest.

O walk with Jesus! To thy view
He will make all things sweet and new;
Will bring new fragrance from each flower,
And hallow every passing hour.

Jesus, a great desire have we
To walk life's troubled path with Thee:
Come to us now, in converse stay;
And O walk with us day by day!

Edwin Paxton Hood
1820–85

Lord, it is such a blessing to know that You want to walk along with us each day. Thank You that we can count on Your presence on our journey through life.

Guard us, guide us, help us, and use us to bring glory to You.

Personal Reflections

Walking in love

'… Love the Lord your God with all your heart
and with all your soul and with all your mind. …
Love your neighbour as yourself.'
Matthew 22:37,39

A s I was driving home one morning after a blessed time of fellowship at a friend's home, the words of an old hymn came into my mind and caused me to burst into song:

Give me a sight, O Saviour,
of thy wondrous love to me,
of the love that brought thee down to earth
to die on Calvary.

O make me understand it,
help me to take it in;
what it meant to thee,
the Holy One,
to bear away my sin.

Was it the nails, O Saviour,
that bound thee to that tree?
Nay, 'twas thine everlasting love,
thy love for me, for me …

Katherine Agnes May Kelly
1869–1942

Our Bible study group had been studying Paul's letter to the Colossians and sharing some thoughts on the love of God. It had occurred to us that so often when we pray for people (and perhaps most particularly for our children whom we long to see totally surrendered to the Lord), we in fact tend to 'major on minors'. We ask for things that are secondary, rather than concentrating on what is most important and fundamental. We pray that they may go to a particular gathering, or be involved in a certain activity, rather than that their basic needs may be met. We commented that, if they truly loved the Lord and gave Him first place in their lives, all those other peripheral things would fall into place.

But how can they (or we!) really come to love the Lord in this way? Is it not only as we begin to understand something of God's love for us that we can then start loving Him in return? That is surely why the apostle Paul prayed the following prayer for the Ephesians: '... I pray that you, being rooted and established in love, may have power ... to grasp how wide and long and high and deep is the love of Christ' (Eph. 3:17).

Love for God and love for others is closely linked in Scripture. Many years ago, in the early 1970s, the years during which our children were being born, we lived in an apartment building in France near the Swiss border. People from the church would come across with meals, offers of help and gifts for the children. One of our neighbours had obviously noticed what had been going on and, amazed, remarked to me on the love that was being shown to us by our Christian friends.

Probably many of us have benefited from the love of our brothers and sisters in Christ in a variety of practical ways – a meal in times of illness, transportation, babysitting ... There are many ways of expressing love in action. Some years ago, Laura, one of our church members, had to go to the hospital every day for radiotherapy. We took it in turns to drive her there. One day the nurse remarked on all these different people who accompanied her. 'Oh! They're all my brothers and sisters!' said Laura.

'... love one another deeply, from the heart' wrote the apostle Peter (1 Pet. 1:22). And Jesus said, 'Love the Lord your God ... Love your neighbour ...' (Matt. 22:37,39). As our love for God grows, so our relationships are transformed. The apostle John exhorts us to '… love one another, for love comes from God' (1 John 4:7). In fact, our love for one another is proof of our love for the Lord. Jesus said, 'As I have loved you, so you must love one another. By this all men will know that you are my disciples, if you love one another' (John 13:34–35).

> *[The Father's] command is that you walk in love.*
> 2 John 6

Thank You, Lord, for loving me so much that You died for me. Thank You, too, that I have so often seen Your love expressed through others. Forgive my selfishness, Lord. Help me to love others in practical ways that will reflect Your love.

Walking in love

Forsaken, Lord? Rejected too?
The spotless Lamb of God?
Abandoned by the Father
Who did not spare the rod?

Insulted, Lord? Misunderstood?
Disowned by friends so dear?
Betrayed for silver pieces
And mocked as men drew near?

Why was it, Lord? Why did you die
Upon the cross that way? –
Despised, hated, insulted –
What penalty to pay?

Redemption, Lord? The price of sin?
You died instead of me?
So I might know the fullness
Of life from sin set free?

I thank you, Lord, for this new life,
For vict'ry over sin,
For love, joy, peace, forgiveness
Since Jesus entered in.

I, too, Lord am rejected now,
Misunderstood like you,
Falsely accused and hated,
Despised, forsaken too.

And yet your Word tells me to love,
To be at peace with men,
To share their joy and sorrow,
Their happiness and pain.

To love and not to count the cost:
I want to do your will.
Help me to obey your Word,
Your purposes fulfil.

Personal Reflections

Walking in hope

Blessed is he … whose hope is in the LORD *his God*
Psalm 146:5

I wonder if you have ever hurt a dear friend. Have you ever let down someone you cared for? What pain you must have felt to know that you were the cause of suffering in one you loved. Peter was an intimate friend of Jesus. Of all the disciples, Peter, James and John were the ones closest to Him. And yet we know that, under extreme pressure, Peter denied Jesus (Matt. 26:69–75). What must he have felt to have disowned his Lord?

We know that Peter '… went outside and wept bitterly' (Matt. 26:75). He had denied knowing his Friend, his Saviour, his Master, his Lord. He must have experienced agony to an extreme degree.

But Peter had a redeeming God. And so do we. If we did not know that we have a God who forgives and can bring good out of evil and who can redeem any situation, we could so easily fall into the depths of despair. God did a transforming work in Peter and equipped him for service. And this same God is transforming us. There is hope for us just as there was for Peter.

Peter's denial was followed by a threefold confession: 'you know that I love you' (see John 21:15–17). The suffering, the pain, the agony, produced a greater love for his Lord. In the same way God can use your painful experience to purify, strengthen and deepen your love for Him and for others. There is always hope in Him.

It was this same Peter who later wrote these wonderfully affirming words that are full of hope: 'Praise be to the God and Father of our Lord Jesus Christ! In his great mercy he has given us new birth into a living hope through the resurrection of Jesus Christ from the dead, and into an inheritance that can never perish, spoil or fade – kept in heaven for you' (1 Pet. 1:3–4).

Often when *we* talk about hope, what we mean is some tentative form of wishful thinking. 'I hope so,' we say without conviction. But when the Bible talks about hope, it is a certainty, an assurance. 'Put your hope in God', says the psalmist in Psalm 42:5. God will never let us down. We can always count on Him. The Bible talks about '... the hope of eternal life ...' (Titus 1:2). This is a certainty, which every believer in Jesus Christ is looking forward to. How bleak life would be if there were no hope.

'... we rejoice in the hope of the glory of God' wrote Paul to the Romans. '... we also rejoice in our sufferings, because we know that suffering produces perseverance; perseverance, character; and character, hope. And hope does not disappoint us ...' (Rom. 5:2–5a).

May the God of hope fill you with all joy and peace as you
trust in him, so that you may overflow with hope by the power
of the Holy Spirit.
Romans 15:13

My hope is built on nothing less
Than Jesus' blood and righteousness;
I dare not trust the sweetest frame,
But wholly lean on Jesus' name.

Edward Smote
1797–1874

Hope

What is this hope the Christian has?
Does he not share the lot of man –
The pain, the suffering, the night,
Injustices we all must fight?

What of his peace amid the pain?
No sign of torment, anguish here,
But quiet acceptance, e'en delight.
Is he not conscious of his plight?

He dwells upon another plane
And faces life with greater strength.
Darkness for him gives way to light:
He lives by faith and not by sight –

Faith in the promises of God
Who for our good spares not the rod.

Thank You, Lord, for the hope that we have in You, which is in fact a blessed assurance. Thank You that we can always count on You. You will never let us down. Thank You that we can look beyond the difficulties of this life to the hope of spending eternity in Your presence.

Personal Reflections

Walking in a spirit of forgiveness

*'… if you forgive men when they sin against you, your heavenly
Father will also forgive you. But if you do not forgive men their sins,
your Father will not forgive your sins.'*
Matthew 6:14–15

How often do we hear on the News, or even in the street and all around us, of conflict, hatred and a desire for revenge? If evil is done to you, then retaliate by giving as good as you get. Stand up for your rights. Your honour is at stake. We seem to have an acute sense of justice – especially when we are personally wronged – and we are quick to retaliate, to hit back and condemn.

In May 2004 we received news from missionary friends of ours who had recently returned home to the USA from the Ivory Coast where there was fighting and unrest. They shared in their letter about a couple there who had 'succeeded in getting Christian pastors from both sides of the ethnic conflict to meet together and pledge to refuse violence but instead to work for reconciliation and peace. Violence and war as a means of trying to settle conflicts leave terrible human wreckage in their wake. Jesus' promise of blessing to the peacemakers takes on profound meaning in situations like this'.

Nowhere, I think, is the Christian message so radically opposed to the way of the world than in the area of forgiveness. 'Make sure that nobody pays back wrong for wrong, but always try to be kind to each other and to everyone else' wrote Paul to the Thessalonians (1 Thess. 5:15). And to the Romans he wrote: 'Bless those who persecute you; bless and do not curse. ... Do not repay anyone evil for evil ... Do not take revenge ... On the contrary: "If your enemy is hungry, feed him; if he is thirsty, give him something to drink. ..." Do not be overcome by evil, but overcome evil with good' (Rom. 12:14,17,19–21).

By those words Paul was endorsing the teaching of Jesus, who said '... Love your enemies, do good to those who hate you, bless those who curse you ...' (Luke 6:27–28). 'But that's not normal!' we might be tempted to exclaim. No, it is not something we would do naturally, but if we profess to follow Jesus, we will obey His teaching. Jesus Himself set us an example: 'When he was abused, he did not return abuse; when he suffered, he did not threaten; but he entrusted himself to the one who judges justly' (1 Pet. 2:23, NRSV).

In Matthew's Gospel chapter 18, Peter is recorded asking Jesus a specific question about forgiveness: '"Lord, how many times shall I forgive my brother when he sins against me? Up to seven times?" Jesus answered, "I tell you, not seven times, but seventy-seven times"' (Matt. 18:21–22). In His reply to Peter the Lord makes it clear that we must forgive not once, or twice, or even seven times, but repeatedly.

It is only as we realise how much God has forgiven us that we in turn will be able to forgive others. It is a well-known fact that those who harbour a spirit of hatred and revenge in their heart are the ones who will suffer most as these negative emotions begin to fester. So for our own good as well as for harmonious relationships, walking in a spirit of forgiveness is the path that we must take.

Jesus said, 'Father, forgive them, for they do not know what they are doing.'
Luke 23:34a

Jesus told Peter a parable to explain how important it is that we forgive one another:

> 'The kingdom of God is like a king who decided to square accounts with his servants. As he got under way, one servant was brought before him who had run up a debt of a hundred thousand dollars. He couldn't pay up, so the king ordered the man, along with his wife, children, and goods, to be auctioned off at the slave market. The poor wretch threw himself at the king's feet and begged, "Give me a chance and I'll pay it all back". Touched by his plea, the king let him off, erasing the debt.
>
> 'The servant was no sooner out of the room when he came upon one of his fellow servants who owed him ten dollars. He seized him by the throat and demanded, "Pay up. Now!"
>
> 'The poor wretch threw himself down and begged, "Give me a chance and I'll pay it all back." But he wouldn't do it. He had him arrested and put in jail until the debt was paid. When the other servants saw this going on, they were outraged and brought a detailed report to the king.
>
> 'The king summoned the man and said, "You evil servant! I forgave your entire debt when you begged me for mercy. Shouldn't you be compelled to be merciful to your fellow servant who asked for mercy?" The king was furious and put the screws to the man until he paid back his entire debt. And that's exactly what my Father in heaven is going to do to each one of you who doesn't forgive unconditionally anyone who asks for mercy.'
>
> Matthew 18:23–35, *The Message*

Lord, You know how difficult it is for us to face injustice. Our instinctive reaction is to hit back, to retaliate. We need a deep work of Your Spirit within us to make us like Jesus. Help us to trust You, Lord, and to forgive, and to respond in love to those who wrong us in any way.

Personal Reflections

_____

_____

_____

_____

_____

_____

_____

_____

_____

_____

_____

_____

_____

_____

_____

_____

_____

_____

_____

_____

_____

_____

_____

_____

_____

_____

_____

Walking in humility

Humble yourselves before the Lord, and he will lift you up.
James 4:10

B
ill, a top executive and successful businessman, was a member of our church. After a fellowship meal or other activity, who would we see sweeping the hall or cleaning up? Yes, you've guessed – Bill. Because of his humility and consistent Christian living and because – as one person who was converted through Bill's testimony put it, 'He lived out Monday through Saturday what he was on Sunday', people were drawn to Jesus.

Bill set us all a good example. So did his Master. In John's Gospel chapter 13, we read that Jesus '… got up from the meal' that He was eating with His disciples, 'took off his outer clothing, and wrapped a towel round his waist'.

> After that, he poured water into a basin and began to wash his disciples' feet, drying them with the towel that was wrapped round him. … When he had finished washing their feet, he put on his clothes and returned to his place. 'Do you understand what I have done for you?' he asked them. 'You call me "Teacher" and "Lord", and rightly so, for that is what I am. Now that I, your Lord and Teacher, have washed your feet, you also should wash one another's feet. I have set you an example that you should do as I have done for you.'
>
> John 13:4–5,12–15

Here we have a supreme example of humility and service shown to the early disciples and to us by our 'Lord and Teacher', the Son of God Himself.

This humble act of service leaves no room for pride and hierarchy. Why didn't one of the disciples perform the traditional foot-washing? Probably because they all expected a servant to do it, which would have been customary. But no servant appeared. Even if it didn't occur to them to wash each other's feet, couldn't one of them at least have washed the feet of their Master? But no, it is the Master Himself who gets up and washes and dries the feet of men who thought themselves above such a menial task.

What an impact this visual aid must have had upon them! What an acted-out lesson in humility and servanthood! And, as if that weren't clear enough, just in case they didn't get the message, Jesus states explicitly, 'you also should wash one another's feet. I have set you an example ...' (John 13:14–15). Let us seek to follow His example and His teaching. Let us walk in humility.

'... clothe yourselves with humility towards one another,' wrote Peter, 'because, "God opposes the proud but gives grace to the humble." Humble yourselves, therefore, under God's mighty hand, that he may lift you up in due time' (1 Pet. 5:5–6).

> '... whoever exalts himself will be humbled,
> and whoever humbles himself will be exalted.'
> Matthew 23:12

Thank You, Lord, for humbling Yourself. Thank You for becoming man and for reaching out in love and humility to those around You. Thank You for the example You have given us. Forgive my pride. Transform me, Lord. Help me to love and serve others, for in so doing I know that I will be loving and serving You. Help me to walk in humility.

Humility

He will be great.
Luke 1:32

'Great will he be'
The angel said.
Great? What does it mean?
He who was led
As lamb to slaughter –
No greatness here.

'Great will he be'.
True God made man.
Great? Rather a slave
Who soon began
To serve his brothers.
No greatness here.

'Great will he be'.
How is this so?
Great? He gave his life
For sin and woe.
Is this not defeat?
No greatness here.

True greatness then?
A life of love,
Of humble service,
Born from above,
Crucifying self.
Real greatness here!

Let the same mind be in you that was in Christ Jesus,
who, though he was in the form of God,
did not regard equality with God
as something to be exploited,
but emptied himself,
taking the form of a slave,
being born in human likeness.
And being found in human form,
he humbled himself
and became obedient to the point of death –
even death on a cross.
Therefore God also highly exalted him
and gave him the name
that is above every name,
so that at the name of Jesus
every knee should bend,
in heaven and on earth and under the earth,
and every tongue should confess
that Jesus Christ is Lord,
to the glory of God the Father.
Philippians 2:5–11, NRSV

Personal Reflections

Walking in trust

Commit your way to the Lord;
trust in him, and he will act.
Psalm 37:5, NRSV

T his week I received an email from a friend I have known for nearly forty years. We were neighbours in Geneva, Switzerland in the mid-1960s. She wrote to say that she has been diagnosed with terminal cancer and might only have a few months to live. She says,

> I have relinquished my body, this cancer and my destiny to God,
> trusting him to be glorified in my body, whether by life or by death.
> I may have cancer, but cancer doesn't have me. God alone has me!
> We know that nothing, not even cancer, can thwart his will.

She is trusting God.

What kind of problems are you facing? What difficulties or tragedies have come your way? Are you perplexed about your circumstances? What a relief it is to know that God is in control and that we can hand things over to Him. We can leave everything in His hands. And what better hands could they be in than those of the almighty, sovereign God, who is also our heavenly Father who loves us and wants the best for us?

'Trust in the Lord with all your heart and lean not on your own understanding' is the wise advice given to us in the book of Proverbs; 'in all your ways acknowledge him, and he will make your paths straight' (Prov. 3:5–6). Peter writes: 'Cast all your anxiety on him because he cares for you' (1 Pet. 5:7). We sometimes talk about 'dumping on people'. Well, here we are invited to 'dump' on God.

Are you anxious about the future? Seek God's guidance and direction. Trust Him to show you the way to go. The verse 'Commit your way to the LORD; trust in him, and he will act' tells us that God does not remain passive. If we commit our way to Him and trust Him, He will act. He will meet our needs. He will show us what to do. He will lead us in the way we should go. 'Blessed is the man who makes the LORD his trust' says the psalmist (Psa. 40:4), and we learn from the book of Proverbs that 'he who trusts in the LORD will prosper' (Prov. 28:25b).

A mother, sitting at the bedside of her seriously injured son, noted:

> I felt my anxiety levels rising, and the desire to take control of things caused my heart to complain to God. But I knew I had to put things back in his hands again, trust him, respond to whatever he prompted me to do, and trust him to do the rest. Then I sensed his peace and assurance again.

... trust in the LORD.
Psalm 4:5

Dear Lord, sometimes my faith is weak and I find it hard to trust You. But I know that You are completely worthy of my trust. I hand my life over to You, Lord. I want to experience Your peace in my heart. I want to walk in Your ways and do Your will.

I am trusting Thee, Lord Jesus,
Trusting only Thee!
Trusting Thee for full salvation,
Great and free.

I am trusting Thee for pardon,
At Thy feet I bow;
For Thy grace and tender mercy,
Trusting now.

I am trusting Thee for cleansing
In the crimson flood;
Trusting Thee to make me holy,
By Thy blood.

I am trusting Thee for power,
Thine can never fail;
Words which Thou Thyself shalt give me
Must prevail.

I am trusting Thee to guide me,
Thou alone shalt lead;
Every day and hour supplying
All my need.

I am trusting Thee, Lord Jesus;
Never let me fall;
I am trusting Thee for ever,
And for all.

Frances Ridley Havergal
1836–79

Personal Reflections

Walking in God's mercy and grace

... because of his great love for us, God, who is rich in mercy, made us alive with Christ even when we were dead in transgressions – it is by grace you have been saved.

Ephesians 2:4–5

I wonder if you have ever had a traffic fine. In Geneva, where I used to spend a lot of my time, traffic fines tripled a few years ago. I then committed a driving offence! Oh! I admitted to being in the wrong and was prepared to take the consequences. At least, I would have been had the amount not been so exorbitant! So I asked for mercy. I appealed to the Swiss police. I appealed to the traffic authorities. I appealed to a court of law. All to no avail. I was guilty. I had to pay the price for transgressing Swiss law.

How different things are with God. Sure, the price had to be paid for my sin. But God, in His mercy and grace, took it upon Himself, in the Person of Jesus Christ, to pay that price. 'For the wages of sin is death' wrote Paul (Rom. 6:23a), and Jesus died in my place. He died so that I might live.

'For by the sacrificial death of Christ we are set free, that is, our sins are forgiven. How great is the grace of God, which he gave to us in such large measure!' (Eph. 1:7–8, GNB; see Bible footnote); I am 'justified freely by [God's] grace' (Rom. 3:24); '... now you have received mercy' wrote Peter (1 Pet. 2:10b).

Paul shares with Timothy how grateful he is to be a beneficiary of God's mercy and grace: 'Even though I was once a blasphemer and a persecutor and a violent man, I was shown mercy because I acted in ignorance and

unbelief. The grace of our Lord was poured out on me abundantly ...'
(1 Tim. 1:13–14a).

I have a friend who has served a prison sentence for a crime he committed. He repented sincerely of the wrong he did and, while still regretting the harm he caused, is experiencing, just like Paul, God's mercy and grace. No one is beyond the mercy of God. What hope this gives us! For no matter how reprehensible our sin, God extends to us His mercy and grace.

Mercy and grace go hand in hand, the opposite sides of the same coin – the first, withholding from us the punishment we deserve; the second, lavishly bestowing on us blessings we do not deserve. God, who paid the penalty for our sin, extends His mercy and grace to us today, so that we might know the joy and freedom of sins forgiven.

> *Let us then approach the throne of grace with confidence,*
> *so that we may receive mercy*
> *and find grace to help us in our time of need.*
> Hebrews 4:16

Thank You, Lord, for Your mercy and Your grace. Thank You for dying for me. Thank You for forgiving my sins. Thank You for the gift of salvation in Jesus.

> *Surely goodness and mercy shall follow me all the days of my life;*
> *and I shall dwell in the house of the LORD for ever.*
> Psalm 23:6, RSV

Amazing grace – how sweet the sound –
That saved a wretch like me!
I once was lost, but now am found,
Was blind, but now I see.

'Twas grace that taught my heart to fear,
And grace my fears relieved;
How precious did that grace appear,
The hour I first believed!

Through many dangers, toils and snares
I have already come:
'Tis grace that brought me safe thus far,
And grace will lead me home.

John Newton
1725–1807

Father, Thine everlasting grace
Our scanty thoughts surpasses far,
Thy heart still melts with tenderness,
Thy arms of love still open are
Returning sinners to receive,
That mercy they may taste and live.

Johann Andreas Rother (1688–1758),
translated by John Wesley (1703–91)

Personal Reflections

Walking in discipline

… the Lord disciplines those whom he loves
Hebrews 12:6a, NRSV

I go to a gym class. Some of the exercises are hard to do. They cause aches and pains and require an effort to accomplish. But they are good for us! Their purpose is to help keep our bodies in good shape. The regular discipline and exercise is beneficial. We laugh a lot too!

Discipline. Not a very popular concept. Painful, undesirable, constricting, discipline goes against the grain and our natural inclination to laziness. The very word conjures up half-forgotten memories of strict teachers at school dispensing sanctions, or of severe parents punishing their offspring for wrongdoing. Discipline is definitely something we could do without.

Is it really? The Bible seems to indicate otherwise. Hebrews chapter 12 has a lot to say about discipline:

… you have forgotten the exhortation that addresses you as children:

'My child, do not regard lightly the
discipline of the Lord,
or lose heart when you are
punished by him;
for the Lord disciplines those whom he loves,
and chastises every child whom he accepts.'

Endure trials for the sake of discipline. God is treating you as children; for what child is there whom a parent does not discipline?

If you do not have that discipline in which all children share, then you are illegitimate and not his children. Moreover, we had human parents to discipline us, and we respected them. Should we not be even more willing to be subject to the Father of spirits and live? For they disciplined us for a short time as seemed best to them, but he disciplines us for our good, in order that we may share his holiness. Now, discipline always seems painful rather than pleasant at the time, but later it yields the peaceful fruit of righteousness to those who have been trained by it.

Hebrews 12:5–11, NRSV

True, it does say that no discipline seems pleasant *at the time* (Heb. 12:11, my italics); but if the discipline itself is painful, let us then focus rather on its results, and see if it is not worth it in the long run.

We have all been around undisciplined children – and maybe suffered the consequences of their bad behaviour! Lack of discipline leads to lack of respect. Parents who lovingly and firmly discipline their children will earn their respect (see Heb. 12:9).

In the above passage it is '… the discipline of the Lord …' (Heb. 12:5, NRSV) that the writer is referring to. That makes all the difference, for even though our human parents disciplined us as they thought best (see v.10), they were not perfect. Neither are we! But we know that the Lord is perfectly just and loving. In fact, the Lord disciplines us *because* He loves us (v.6). His discipline is the proof that we are His children (vv.7–8). And His discipline is never arbitrary, but always purposeful and constructive. It is 'for our good, in order that we may share his holiness' (v.10, NRSV). Even though it is painful while we are going through it, 'later it yields the peaceful fruit of righteousness to those who have been trained by it' (v.11, NRSV). So, discipline is part of God's training programme to make us holy and righteous; in other words, to make us like Jesus.

He disciplines us for our good.
Hebrews 12:10, NRSV

Discipline

Just keep your eyes on the Saviour
And never forget his love.
Don't look at human behaviour
But focus on him above.

Tell him your heartache and grieving
Then ask him to meet your need,
And when the waters start seething
Just follow your Saviour's lead.

He will protect in the danger –
Don't be afraid of the waves,
This erstwhile babe in the manger
Is Jesus – the One who saves.

Human emotions are draining.
Perception is often dim.
Let's see the hard times as training –
Preparing for life with him.

Thank You, Lord, that I am Your child and that You love me enough to
discipline me. I thank You that through it You are training me, so that I
will become more like Jesus. Help me to see my trials in this perspective.

Personal Reflections

Walking by the Spirit

… walk by the Spirit, and do not gratify the desires of the flesh. …
Galatians 5:16, RSV

I t is Ascension weekend as I write this week's meditation. I have just been sitting in a sheltered corner of our terrace, bathed in the warmth of the golden evening sunlight, while all around me a chilly wind blows in gusts, rustling the leaves in the trees and bending the top-most branches of a tall poplar. It reminds me of Jesus' words to Nicodemus: 'The wind blows wherever it pleases. You hear its sound, but you cannot tell where it comes from or where it is going. So it is with everyone born of the Spirit' (John 3:8).

In France, where I live, Ascension Day, which always falls on a Thursday in spring, is a public holiday. Many people, however, do not know the significance of it, even though it is one of the most popular holidays in France, due to the fact that those who can, take the Friday off too, thus making it into a long weekend. It unfortunately also has the sad reputation of being the weekend with the most road accidents.

But why do we celebrate Ascension Day? It is the day when Jesus went back to heaven after His life on earth. He had prepared His disciples very carefully for this moment, but even so, they could not help being 'filled with grief' (see John 16:6). Jesus even said to them: 'It is for your good that I am going away' (John 16:7a). How could that possibly be? He explained: 'Unless I go away, the Counsellor will not come to you; but if I go, I will send him to you' (John 16:7b). And Jesus tells them that this Counsellor will be with them forever (see John 14:16). Not only will He be *with* them, but He will also be *in* them (see John 14:17).

Who is the Counsellor and what is His role? Jesus explained to His disciples that the Counsellor is none other than the Holy Spirit, the third Person of the Trinity, and that He would remind them of Jesus' teaching (see John 14:26). He would testify about Jesus (John 15:26), and also give the disciples power to witness (see John 15:27; Acts 1:8).

'Well,' you might be tempted to say, 'that must have been great for those early disciples, but I don't really see how it concerns me.' This glorious truth is for every Christian, because each of us is indwelt by God's Spirit. He is at work within us just as He was in the lives of Jesus' first disciples. He gives us the strength to live for God in a world that is hostile to Him. He can give us the power to resist temptation.

Do you sometimes feel lonely and discouraged? Take heart! You are never alone. Jesus is with you in the Person of His Spirit. Do you sometimes despair of ever being able to reach people with the gospel? Take courage! Count on the power of the Holy Spirit to enable you to be an effective witness.

'… be filled with the Spirit' wrote Paul to the Ephesians (5:18b). If we are filled with the Spirit, we will show forth the fruit of the Spirit in our lives – love, joy, peace, patience, kindness, goodness, faithfulness, gentleness and self-control (Gal. 5:22–23a) – and so glorify Jesus Christ and please our Father in heaven who sent the Spirit to us.

> *If we live by the Spirit, let us also walk by the Spirit.*
> Galatians 5:25a, RSV

Lord, I want to reflect Jesus in all that I do and am. Please put Your finger on any part of my life that does not glorify You. Reveal to me any inconsistencies and help me to correct them. Thank You for Your Holy Spirit who indwells me. Lord, I want to be filled with Your Spirit and controlled by Him. May the fruit of the Spirit be evidenced in my life.

As I looked round at the members of our church, met together to worship God, I prayed this prayer:

Walking by the Spirit

Lord, may your Spirit
Sweep in cleansing breath
Across your children gathered here,
Purifying,
Sanctifying,
Disciplining,
Turning our thoughts heavenward.

For how can we hope to please you, Lord,
Obsessed as we are with things:
Possessions,
Job,
Status.

Give us the mind of him,
Who divine, yet became man,
Humbling himself unto death,
Yes, even death on the cross.

Personal Reflections

Walking in the truth

'I am the way and the truth and the life.
No-one comes to the Father except through me.'
John 14:6

The year 1998 saw the end of compulsory military service in France. Our younger son was one of the last conscripts to perform this duty for his country. Just as he shrank from joining the artillery regiment to which he was assigned, so we get the impression that a timid young man named Timothy may have baulked at entering the spiritual battle to which he was called.

The apostle Paul gave him instructions and expected him to follow them: 'Timothy, my son, I give you this instruction in keeping with the prophecies once made about you, so that by following them you may fight the good fight, holding on to faith and a good conscience' (1 Tim. 1:18–19a). Paul tells him in no uncertain terms that it is his duty to 'fight'.

Contrary to many battles being waged today, Timothy was to 'fight the *good* fight' (my italics). What is this 'good fight' he was to be engaged in? A little earlier, Paul had referred to the wrong teaching that was being propagated. It would seem, therefore, that Timothy was to fight for the truth in the face of error. '… stay there in Ephesus' wrote Paul, 'so that you may command certain men not to teach false doctrines any longer' (1 Tim. 1:3).

Just as our son was handed a rifle on entering his regiment, so Timothy had weapons made available to him. His two weapons – 'faith and a good conscience' – go very much hand in hand, the latter being dependent on the former. Right living stems from sound doctrine.

Towards the end of his letter, Paul again uses the same expression, 'Fight the good fight …' (1 Tim. 6:12a). This time it seems to be more in a moral context, as Paul also mentioned the 'ruin and destruction' (1 Tim. 6:9) that can come upon those who have an inordinate love of riches. So whether doctrine or practice is at stake, Timothy is to 'Fight the good fight of the faith' (1 Tim. 6:12a).

And so are we. We are to stand up for the truth in the face of false teaching. We are to 'pursue righteousness, godliness, faith, love, endurance and gentleness' (1 Tim. 6:11) in a world that is greedy for wealth. We are to walk in the truth of the teaching of God's Word. '… love truth and peace' exhorts the prophet Zechariah (8:19).

John has much to say about our walk with God in this context of truth and falsehood. In his second letter, writing to warn a young church of the danger of itinerant false teachers, he rejoices over some of the members who are '… walking in the truth …' (2 John 4). He picks up on this again in his third letter: 'It gave me great joy to have some brothers come and tell about your faithfulness to the truth and how you continue to walk in the truth. I have no greater joy than to hear that my children are walking in the truth' (3 John 3–4).

As we approach the end of our spring readings and prepare to launch into our summer themes, let us determine to walk in the truth as revealed to us in God's Word.

I have chosen the way of truth …
Psalm 119:30

Come, my Way, my Truth, my Life:
Such a Way, as gives us breath:
Such a Truth, as ends all strife:
Such a Life as killeth death.

George Herbert
1593–1633

Teach me your way, O LORD,
and I will walk in your truth …
Psalm 86:11a

Yes Lord, You are the way and the truth and the life. Please keep me faithfully walking in Your ways and in the truth. May my life be firmly grounded in the truth of Your Word. Help me to recognise false teaching and to stand up for the truth.

Personal Reflections

Summer

We read in the Bible that God '... was walking in the garden in the cool of the day ...' (Gen. 3:8). Summer is a time when we welcome warmth and sunshine. In many parts of the world, we also look for shade. We avoid being outside in extreme heat. The ground is parched, and forest fires may ravage the hillsides.

We seek refreshment and green pastures and cool breezes or invigorating mountain air. 'What is more gentle than a wind in summer?' asked John Keats (1795–1821). We anticipate a slower pace of life as we take time to rest or enjoy a holiday and leisure activities.

Poet James Thomson (1700–48) rightly associates each season with God. After extolling the joy of spring with its 'softening air', he welcomes the warmth of summer:

> Then comes thy glory in the Summer-months,
> With light and heat refulgent. Then thy sun
> Shoots full perfection through the swelling year:
> And oft thy voice in dreadful thunder speaks,
> And oft, at dawn, deep noon, or falling eve,
> By brooks and groves, in hollow-whispering gales.

We continue to walk with God throughout the summer months. As we see the fruit ripening on the trees, and as we anticipate a sense of fulfilment, we walk onwards with renewed energy and with God's help and in His strength, purposefully, in those 'ancient paths' (see Jer. 6:16), towards the goal that He has set for us.

Walking closely

Come near to God and he will come near to you.
James 4:8a

O n 2 September 1998, flight SR111 from New York to Geneva attempted an emergency landing on the sea near Halifax, Nova Scotia. Of the 220 passengers on board, there were no survivors. For those of us in Geneva, the crash hit very close to home. All of us were shocked. Whether personally bereaved or not, we were all very aware that 'it could so easily have been me'.

Whether we escaped by the skin of our teeth, as it were, through cancelling a previously-made booking on that same flight, or whether we had no plans at all for travel just then, the fact is that 'we who are still alive and are left' (1 Thess. 4:17) are here on earth for a purpose. We need to find out what that purpose is.

'What is the chief end of man?' asks The Shorter Catechism, which then goes on to give the answer: 'To glorify God and to enjoy him forever'. Those who know the Lord and have assurance of eternal life have the responsibility to share the gospel – the good news – with others.

Those who have not yet entered into a personal relationship with God through Jesus Christ, who do not know the joy of sins forgiven, who have never walked closely with Him, still have the opportunity to turn to Him in repentance and faith and receive His gift of salvation.

Paul wrote: '… now is the time of God's favour, now is the day of salvation' (2 Cor. 6:2). Sobering words from the writer of the letter to the Hebrews remind us that '… man is destined to die once, and after that to face judgment' (Heb. 9:27).

If this plane crash, or others that have occurred since, or the September 11 terrorist attacks on the Twin Towers in New York in 2001, or the Bali bombing in October 2002 or the Madrid bombings on 11 March 2004, or those in London on 7 July 2005 or subsequent attacks elsewhere, or some other tragedy, could only motivate us all to seek the Lord, to draw close to Him, then surely out of horror could spring forth hope.

As this book has developed, I have often stopped to think what it really means to walk closely with God. I hope that what you read serves to encourage you to draw close to Him. When we do, we know that He also draws close to us. 'Come near to God, and he will come near to you' writes James (4:8a, GNB).

Walking with Him means living out a close relationship with Him, talking to Him, listening to Him, knowing who He is, knowing what He is like, quite simply knowing *Him*. The verb 'to know', as it is used in the Scriptures implies intimacy. This is the kind of relationship we can have with God through Jesus. Remember how pleased Jesus was when Mary chose to be close to Him and to listen to Him (Luke 10:38–42).

Walking with Him also means taking note of His Word and living in the light of His promises. I pray that all who read this book will be encouraged to walk closely with Him in an increasing depth of relationship and trust.

Cast all your anxiety on him because he cares for you.
1 Peter 5:7

Oh! for a closer walk with God

Oh! for a closer walk with God,
A calm and heav'nly frame;
A light to shine upon the road
That leads me to the Lamb!

Where is the blessedness I knew
When first I saw the Lord?
Where is the soul-refreshing view
Of Jesus, and his word?

What peaceful hours I once enjoy'd!
How sweet their mem'ry still!
But they have left an aching void,
The world can never fill.

Return, O holy Dove, return,
Sweet messenger of rest;
I hate the sins that made thee mourn,
And drove thee from my breast.

The dearest idol I have known,
Whate'er that idol be;
Help me to tear it from thy throne,
And worship only thee.

So shall my walk be close with God,
Calm and serene my frame;
So purer light shall mark the road
That leads me to the Lamb.

William Cowper
1731–1800

Thank You, Lord, that You want to be in relationship with Your children. Thank You that we can call You 'Father'. I want to draw close to You, Lord, and I know that if I do, then You will also draw close to me. Thank You that I can walk through life in close fellowship with You, with my sins forgiven, because of the work of Jesus at the cross.

Personal Reflections

Walking onwards

... you will go on your way in safety, and your foot will not stumble.
Proverbs 3:23

A friend in Oregon once asked me to tell her about my 'inner journey'. After the initial surprise had passed and as I reflected further, the thought came to me that as Christians indwelt by the Spirit of the living God our 'inner journey' will of necessity be inextricably interwoven with our relationship to Jesus Christ. As we enter into a deeper experience of Christ, as we grow in our knowledge of Him and of God's Word, as we come to love Him more, so we are journeying on.

But what of our destination? Some years ago, as my husband and I travelled in the south-west of the United States, where vast hot deserts give way to cooler mountain passes and where steep, rocky cliffs meet sandy beaches, we knew each day where we were heading. Even before we set off, our destination had been planned.

What about our walk through life? Do we know where we are going? Or are we wandering about in a fog of uncertainty? The Bible tells us that 'There is a way that seems right to a man, but in the end it leads to death' (Prov. 14:12). And God says to His people: '... I have set before you life and death ... Now choose life ...' (Deut. 30:19).

When Thomas asked Jesus '... how can we know the way?' Jesus replied, 'I am the way and the truth and the life' (John 14:5–6). Let us walk through life with Him. He will lead us to our final destination, that 'city' mentioned in Hebrews 11:16, which God has prepared for us.

In Genesis 12:8 we are told that Abram 'pitched his tent'. What does this mean in spiritual terms? How can we live in tents, metaphorically speaking, today in our ultra-sophisticated, highly materialistic western society? Hebrews chapter 11 gives us some indication of the wealth of meaning behind this simple expression, Abram 'pitched his tent'. We read,

> By faith Abraham, when called to go to a place he would later receive as his inheritance, obeyed and went, even though he did not know where he was going. By faith he made his home in the promised land like a stranger in a foreign country; he lived in tents … For he was looking forward to the city with foundations, whose architect and builder is God.
>
> Heb. 11:8–10

We are told that Abraham lived 'like a stranger in a foreign country'. Have you ever lived in a foreign country? If so, you probably felt as if you did not really belong there. Your roots did not go down very far. You may have found it difficult to identify with local customs and culture and relate to what was going on around you. You did not speak the language. You did not feel 'at home'.

John writes: 'We know that we are God's children, and that the whole world lies under the power of the evil one' (1 John 5:19, NRSV). Is it surprising, then, that a Christian living in this world might also feel 'like a stranger in a foreign country'? We are 'aliens and strangers on earth' (Heb. 11:13). Like those mentioned in Hebrews 11:16, we are 'longing for a better country – a heavenly one'. Let us not put our roots down here too firmly or too deeply. We have to move on. After all, 'our citizenship is in heaven' (Phil. 3:20).

Now we know that if the earthly tent we live in is destroyed,
we have a building from God, an eternal house in heaven, not
built by human hands.
2 Corinthians 5:1

Walking onwards

Open my eyes, Lord, to see,
As Elisha did,
Your mighty army encompassing me.
Help me to look beyond
The world physical,
The world material
And not only to look but to live.

To live on this other plane.

Are we not told
The visible will pass away
But the invisible last forever?
Perspective, Lord, is what we need,
A right perspective.
Thank you for the gift
Of enjoying eternity here and now.

Lord, I realise that it is very easy to become attached to the things of this world. Help me to hold them loosely in my hands. Help me not to put my roots down too firmly or too deep, but to move on in the way that You will show me. Thank You that you are the way, the truth and the life, and that my destination is sure, because You have prepared a place for me.

Personal Reflections

WEEK 16

Walking in God's strength

God is our refuge and strength,
an ever-present help in trouble.
Psalm 46:1

How did you begin this new week? Depressed because of world events? Discouraged through personal failure? Determined that this will be a good week? Desirous to see God's purposes accomplished? Whatever we may feel, vanquished or victorious, let us get one thing straight: we will accomplish nothing of lasting value in our own strength.

Jesus said, '… apart from me you can do nothing' (John 15:5). We cannot change the world, or even a small part of it. We cannot even change ourselves. We do not know what the future may bring. And, as for accomplishing God's purposes, how pretentious!

And yet … and yet … What was it Paul said? 'For when I am weak, then I am strong' (2 Cor. 12:10b) and 'I can do everything through him who gives me strength' (Phil. 4:13). What an absolute reversal of the situation. Nothing without Christ; everything with Christ.

Change the world? Did Jesus not tell His followers they were the light of the world and the salt of the earth (Matt. 5:13–14)? Let our light shine. Let our salt do its purifying work.

Personal failure? Yes, but that is reckoning without 1 John 1:9 – 'If we confess our sins, he is faithful and just and will forgive us our sins and purify us from all unrighteousness.' We can start again, forgiven and cleansed. Not only does He forgive, but also He is the One 'who is able to keep you from falling' (Jude 24).

And what about the future? Do you remember those well-known words, 'I know not what the future holds, but I know who holds the future'? How wonderful to know that our lives are in the hands of our heavenly Father and that we can trust Him.

As for accomplishing God's purposes, what more do we need than the following command and promise: '… All authority in heaven and on earth has been given to me. Therefore go and make disciples of all nations … And surely I am with you always …' (Matt. 28:18–20).

May we never try to live the Christian life in our own strength. We are doomed to failure. Let us walk in God's strength. Our life is in Him. '… your life is now hidden with Christ in God' wrote Paul (Col. 3:3). Let us live it that way! '… be strong in the Lord and in his mighty power' (Eph. 6:10).

> *… God is the strength of my heart …*
> Psalm 73:26

Thank You, Lord, for Your strength, and for reminding me that I can do all things through Christ who strengthens me.

God's strength

Lord,
I want to be yours,
Wholly yours.
Distractions tear me away,
Take up my time,
Occupy my thoughts.

Lord,
To focus on you,
Only you,
That is all my desire,
All that I want,
And all that I need.

Lord,
To live in your strength,
Not my own.
All alone I am weak.
In you I am strong.
I will count on you.

And Lord,
To hear just your voice,
Yours alone.
So many noises around
Want attention,
Shouting to be heard.

Personal Reflections

Walking with God's help

Help, LORD *…*
Psalm 12:1

I had a bit of a setback while I was writing *Paths of Peace*. The problem was directly related to the book. The difficulty caused my mind to go blank and I could think of nothing more to say. I was so discouraged and distressed that I felt like abandoning it and never writing anything again.

Shortly before this, I had been reading through the book of Exodus. In chapters 35–39, we are told how God equipped skilled craftsmen to make the tabernacle and all its furnishings according to His instructions:

> … the LORD has chosen Bezalel … and he has filled him with the
> Spirit of God, with skill, ability and knowledge in all kinds of crafts
> – to make artistic designs for work in gold, silver and bronze, to cut
> and set stones, to work in wood and to engage in all kinds of artistic
> craftsmanship.
>
> Exodus 35:30–33

As I read, I marvelled at the colours – blue, purple and scarlet – and the beauty and the intricacy of the embroidery and the high quality of the materials. I was lost in admiration at the decoration of the lampstand, with its flowers and buds and blossoms, all 'hammered out of pure gold' (Exod. 37:22b). The perfection of the work done in other precious metals and wood and precious stones is also described in detail. When all was completed, 'Moses inspected the work and saw that they had done it just as the LORD had commanded …' (Exod. 39:43). Nothing but the best would do for God. He had provided His people with the gifts and the skill to perfectly accomplish the work in the way He had planned.

I had found this account interesting and fascinating and inspiring, but no more than that. To me, it was an historical event in the lives of God's people, but it did not seem to have any relation or relevance to me. However, as I was out walking one morning and talking to the Lord about the problem I was facing, and sharing with Him the disappointment and sadness I was feeling, He brought to mind those passages in the book of Exodus where we read of the beautiful work those skilled craftsmen had done for Him. It was as if God were saying to me, 'I want you to use the skills I have given you to produce something beautiful for Me. I have given you this gift of words and it is for Me that you are writing this book. You are indwelt by My Spirit. Let Him inspire you.'

I suddenly felt elated at this commission from the Lord. After feeling completely demotivated, my enthusiasm returned and I could hardly get home fast enough to start work on the book again. I am writing for Him, using the skills and the gifts He has given me. I know that I can count on His help as this work develops. I am doing my best for Him. And may all the glory be His!

Surely God is my help;
the Lord is the one who sustains me.
Psalm 54:4

Thank You, Lord, that I can count on Your help. Thank You for encouraging me. Thank You for the gifts and skills You have given me. Help me to produce something beautiful for You.

God's help

The LORD is my rock,
my fortress, and my deliverer ...
my light and my salvation ...
the stronghold of my life ...
my strength and my shield;
in him my heart trusts:
so I am helped
Psalm 18:2a; 27:1; 28:7, NRSV

The Lord is my rock ...
In Him I am on solid ground, a firm foundation. He will keep my feet from slipping.

My fortress ...
In Him I am safe and secure.

And my deliverer ...
Lord, lead me not into temptation, but deliver me from evil and from the tempter's snare.

My light ...
He brought me 'out of darkness into his wonderful light' (1 Pet. 2:9). I must live in the light. '... men loved darkness instead of light because their deeds were evil' (John 3:19).

And my salvation ...
Thank You, Lord, for saving me from sin. I belong to Jesus and I must crucify 'the sinful nature with its passions and desires' (Gal. 5:24).

The stronghold of my life …

He protects me and keeps me steady and firm.

My strength …

I really need Your strength, Lord, in my weakness (see 2 Cor. 12:10b).

And my shield …

Yes, Lord, help me to resist those fiery darts and be victorious over the enemy.

In Him my heart trusts …

Thank You, Lord, that I can just throw myself on You, and lean on You, rely on You, count on You. I need You so much.

So I am helped.

Bring me through, Lord, to the perfect peace and rest that You have promised. Thank You that I can be sure of Your help.

Personal Reflections

Walking purposefully

The path of the righteous is level;
O upright One, you make the way of the righteous smooth.
Isaiah 26:7

L ooking back over my life, I can see how the Lord has led me step by
step. He gave me parents who loved me and cared for me. He drew
me to Himself when I was still a child. He put people on my path
who were instrumental in my spiritual growth. He gave me opportunities
to study and to use the gifts that He has given me. Later, He led my husband
and me into Christian ministry. He continues to give us opportunities of
service. We want to live for Him. That is our purpose in life.

As you examine your life, do you see any clearly-defined goals? Are you
heading in a particular direction? Which paths are you following? Are you
walking purposefully?

In contrast, in Psalm 107, we have a picture of those who are lost and
homeless. 'Some wandered in desert wastelands, finding no way to a city
where they could settle. They were hungry and thirsty, and their lives ebbed
away' (vv.4–5). What a horrible picture of nothingness and lostness.

The city that is mentioned would be a place of refuge, where they would
have been able to settle and put down roots. But, in contrast, they walked
aimlessly. They had no roots, no security, no place to call their own. They
were dying of hunger and thirst and distress. What a scene of hopelessness
and death.

But in their despair they knew where to turn. We read in verse 6: 'Then
they cried out to the LORD in their trouble, and he delivered them from their
distress.' Are you wandering 'in desert wastelands', figuratively speaking,

with no purpose in life? If you find yourself walking aimlessly, with no direction, why not cry out to God for deliverance?

How did God deliver these lost, homeless wanderers? 'He led them by a straight way ...' (v.7), in contrast to all their aimless meanderings. God gave direction to their lives. 'He led them by a straight way to a city where they could settle' (v.7), that place of security where they could put down roots and belong. Under God's leading, they began to walk purposefully.

God created us to be in relation to Himself. We are, however, separated from Him because of our sin and rebellion and our desire to be autonomous. And so, even though we may have ambitious short-term goals, and we may do some good in the world, basically we wander 'in desert wastelands', not knowing which way to turn. We walk aimlessly, with no clear direction in our lives. Cut off from God, we can have no real purpose in living. When Cain sinned, God said to him, 'You will be a restless wanderer on the earth' (Gen. 4:12).

To those wandering in desert wastes who have lost their way, Jesus says, 'I am the way' (John 14:6). To those who are hungry, Jesus says, 'I am the bread of life' (John 6:35). And to those who are thirsty and tired, He is the living water and the giver of rest. He says, 'Come to me, all you who are weary and burdened, and I will give you rest' (Matt. 11:28).

It is only as we come back into a relationship with God through Jesus Christ, that we will become the people God intended us to be. Then our lives will take on a new direction. We will begin to walk purposefully in the ways that God has planned and prepared for us.

Whether you turn to the right or to the left,
your ears will hear a voice behind you,
saying, 'This is the way; walk in it.'
Isaiah 30:21

Teach me Thy way, O Lord,
Teach me Thy way!
Thy gracious aid afford,
Teach me Thy way!
Help me to walk aright;
More by faith, less by sight:
Lead me with heavenly light:
Teach me Thy way!

When doubts and fears arise,
Teach me thy way!
When storms o'erspread the skies,
Teach me Thy way!
Shine through the cloud and rain,
Through sorrow toil and pain;
Make Thou my pathway plain:
Teach me Thy way!

Long as my life shall last,
Teach me Thy way!
Where'er my lot be cast,
Teach me Thy way!
Until the race is run,
Until the journey's done,
Until the crown is won,
Teach me Thy way.

Benjamin Mansell Ramsey
1849–1923

Thank You, Lord, that You give purpose and direction to my life. I want to live for You. Thank You for the gifts You have given me. I want to use them for You. Thank You for leading me in those paths that You have planned and prepared for me.

Personal Reflections

Walking towards the goal

*I press on towards the goal to win the prize for which God
has called me heavenwards in Christ Jesus.*
Philippians 3:14

C elebrations went on all night in France on 12 July 1998. The French
football team had won the World Cup! If I remember correctly,
they scored three goals against Brazil. Each time a goal was scored,
fans went wild: 'It's a goal!'

The following lines are taken from my journal:

Whether I am conscious of it or not, God is the goal or object of my
deepest desires, so why try to find fulfilment in lesser things, even
though these 'lesser things' may be good gifts from my heavenly
Father? May all the gifts point me to the Giver and never become an
end in themselves, even though God has given them to me to enjoy.
He must be my focus. He alone can satisfy, so why seek satisfaction
elsewhere?

This was so much a part of the apostle Paul's thinking that
it didn't make much difference to him whether he was 'in the
body' or 'with Christ' (Philippians 1:23, 24). We know what his
preference was, what he considered to be 'better by far' (Philippians
23b). Sometimes people wonder what they'll be doing in heaven.
Paul says, 'We make it our goal to please him, whether we are at
home in the body or away from it' (2 Corinthians 5:9). It is good
to know that if we make that our goal now, 'down here', it will

also be our goal then, 'up there'. It will not have changed; there will be continuity. I do not want to lose sight of this truth. I am so conscious of my own weakness and inconsistency. But I keep hearing the Lord say, 'My power is made perfect in weakness' (2 Corinthians 12:9). I want to abandon myself completely to him.

Can I truly echo the words of the apostle Paul, 'I consider everything a loss compared to the surpassing greatness of knowing Christ Jesus my Lord' (Philippians 3:8)? Sometimes I feel so discouraged that I am incapable of living out all that I believe. But then I say, 'Well, of course you can't, stupid, nobody said you could live the Christian life in your own strength. It's impossible'! But 'I can do all things through Christ who strengthens me'. Then comes the soul-searching question: 'Do you really want to?' And the honest answer, 'Yes… but maybe not always'. There are earthly pleasures I wish to taste more deeply of. And then I hear in my head: 'Taste and see that *the* Lord *is* good' (Psalm 34:8).

So, sometimes my focus blurs, my goal recedes, my sight grows dim. I can only throw myself on the mercy of the Lord: 'Lord, I believe. Help my unbelief'! Sometimes I feel I'm right back to the beginning again, back to basics. What have I learned and appropriated during the fifty years or so that I have been a Christian?

Yes, we inevitably have times of discouragement. However, we need to persevere. In order to score a goal, or to hit any kind of target, one has to take careful aim. Let us keep our eyes fixed on Jesus (see Heb. 12:2) and '… make it our goal to please him …' (2 Cor. 5:9).

> *Not that I have already … reached the goal; but I press on to make*
> *it my own, because Christ Jesus has made me his own.*
> Philippians 3:12, NRSV

Thy way, not mine

Thy way, not mine, O Lord,
However dark it be!
Lead me by Thine own hand,
Choose out the path for me.

Smooth let it be or rough,
It will be still the best;
Winding or straight, it leads
Right onward to Thy rest.

I dare not choose my lot;
I would not, if I might;
Choose Thou for me, my God;
So shall I walk aright.

The kingdom that I seek
Is Thine; so let the way
That leads to it be Thine;
Else I must surely stray.

Take Thou my cup, and it
With joy or sorrow fill,
As best to Thee may seem;
Choose Thou my good and ill.

Choose thou for me my friends,
My sickness or my health;
Choose Thou my cares for me,
My poverty or wealth.

Not mine, not mine the choice,
In things or great or small;
Be Thou my guide, my strength,
My wisdom, and my all!

Horatius Bonar
1808–89

Thank You, Lord, for all the encouragement we find in Your Word. Thank You for the example of all the believers who have gone before us and who are cheering us on, as it were. Yes, thank You for that 'great cloud of witnesses' (Heb. 12:1). Help us to press on towards the goal. Help us to persevere, in spite of our own weaknesses, and despite discouragements that come our way. Help us to keep our eyes fixed on You, Lord.

Personal Reflections

Walking in wisdom

If any of you lacks wisdom, he should ask God, who gives generously
to all without finding fault, and it will be given to him.
James 1:5

We need wisdom in all areas of our life – in relating with people, in parenting, in business, in running our home, in decision-making, in all of our responsibilities … Let us then remember to ask God for it. How encouraging it is to know that we can count on Him to give us the wisdom we need.

Sometimes when we come to God with our requests, we are not sure that what we are asking is in line with His will for us. We're not sure that our request really corresponds to what would be best or right under the circumstances. However, we need never be reticent about asking God for wisdom. Why? Because if we ask for wisdom, we have the promise that God will answer our prayer. He will give us the wisdom we ask for. James writes in his letter: 'If any of you lacks wisdom, he should ask God … and it will be given to him' (James 1:5). And the book of Proverbs also tells us that '… the LORD gives wisdom' (Prov. 2:6).

When Solomon became king, he asked God for wisdom to govern his people. We read that, 'It pleased the Lord that Solomon had asked this' (1 Kings 3:10, NRSV). 'God gave Solomon very great wisdom, discernment, and breadth of understanding as vast as the sand on the seashore, so that Solomon's wisdom surpassed the wisdom of all the people of the east, and all the wisdom of Egypt. He was wiser than anyone else …' (1 Kings 4:29–31, NRSV).

Paul tells the Colossian Christians to 'Be wise in the way you act towards outsiders; make the most of every opportunity. Let your conversation be always full of grace, seasoned with salt, so that you may know how to answer everyone' (Col. 4:5–6).

In the Scriptures – and in life – wisdom and understanding go hand in hand. 'The fear of the Lord is the beginning of wisdom' we read in Proverbs 9:10 and the verse continues: 'and knowledge of the Holy One is understanding.' In his prayer for the Christians in Colosse, Paul also links wisdom and understanding. He writes: '… we have not stopped praying for you and asking God to fill you with the knowledge of his will through all spiritual wisdom and understanding' (Col. 1:9).

To know God's will is surely what every believer desires. We often pray for guidance in the different – often complex – circumstances of our lives. How affirming it is, then, to read words such as these: 'I guide you in the way of wisdom and lead you along straight paths' (Prov. 4:11).

… he who walks in wisdom is kept safe.
Proverbs 28:26

Thank You, Lord, for the promise that You will give me wisdom if I ask You for it. I need it so much in all areas of my life. Please give me wisdom in my relationships and in my responsibilities.

Wisdom

Lord, I want to welcome each new day,
Open-armed, as a gift from you.
To accept all it brings
And live it to the full,
Live it for you.

And yet there are choices,
Decisions to be made.
Give me wisdom, Lord,
In what to do.
And, perhaps even more,
In what not to do.

And then there are
Needs to be met.
Is it I, Lord, who must go?
When to say 'yes'?
When to say, 'No'?

And what about the joys and pleasures of life?
Do I indulge, or abstain?
Good gifts are from you, Lord,
Pleasures from your right hand.

Sorrows, too, Lord are part of life.
How do I cope? What do I do?
Comfort me, Lord. I need you so!
Give me the strength to praise you too.

And so as I welcome each new day,
I need your wisdom and your grace
To live each moment to the full,
Responsibly and in your will.

Who among you is wise and understanding? Let him show by his good behaviour his deeds in the gentleness of wisdom. But if you have bitter jealousy and selfish ambition in your heart, do not be arrogant and so lie against the truth. This wisdom is not that which comes down from above, but is earthly, natural, demonic. For where jealousy and selfish ambition exist, there is disorder and every evil thing. But the wisdom from above is first pure, then peaceable, gentle, reasonable, full of mercy and good fruits, unwavering, without hypocrisy. And the seed whose fruit is righteousness is sown in peace by those who make peace.
James 3:13–18, NASB

Personal Reflections

Walking patiently

Be still before the Lord
and wait patiently for him …
Psalm 37:7

B e still. Calm down. Stop worrying. Stop getting in a state. 'Be still'
could also be translated here 'Be quiet' … 'Be silent'. Silence is a
rather rare commodity these days. On a TV quiz programme that
I watch, one of the candidates was asked if she was afraid of silence. She
replied, 'Not at all. Silence is necessary for any deep reflection.'

'Be still, and know that I am God' we read in Psalm 46:10:

'Be still' – be quiet, stop agitating, stop fussing, stop fretting, stop all panic
and worry, and just leave it all to Me
'and know' – be aware, recognise, experience, trust, believe
'that I am God' – almighty, all-powerful, all-knowing, holy, loving, wanting
the best for My children, in control, sovereign.

But maybe people who shy away from reflection, who are afraid of hearing
God's 'gentle whisper' (1 Kings 19:12), prefer constant noise so as to block
out anything they don't want to hear. In our noisy world, where people are
always on the go, and where all around us music blares and phones ring
and electronic gadgets beep, it is not easy to find that quiet place to be still
before the Lord.

Why not look for a place where you can spend time in tranquillity in the
Lord's presence? Depending on your circumstances and responsibilities,
this will have to be at the time of day that suits your schedule best. My best

time is early morning, when all is still and quiet, before I launch into the activities of the day.

'Wait patiently' says the verse quoted above. Which of us likes to wait? Not very many people that I know! We are normally very *im*patient. (Maybe I should speak for myself!). But the psalmist encourages us to wait patiently *for Him*, for the Lord. God will act. Yes, but when? In His own time, the right time, the best time.

Whenever the Bible tells us to wait, it is never a passive resignation that is meant, but rather an active, eager, expectant anticipation. Are you waiting for an answer to prayer? Well, 'Be still before the LORD and wait patiently for him'. Are you waiting to see some positive outcome from the trials you are going through? 'Be still before the LORD and wait patiently for him'.

> *I waited patiently for the LORD;*
> *he turned to me and heard my cry.*
> Psalm 40:1

Lord, You know how hard it is for me to be patient. Everything seems to go so fast these days. Waiting is hard. But I want to trust You, Lord. I know that You will act when the time is right, so help me just to leave all my concerns with You and wait patiently.

Patience taught by Nature

'O dreary life', we cry, 'O dreary life!'
And still the generations of the birds
Sing through our sighing, and the flocks and herds
Serenely live while we are keeping strife
With Heaven's true purpose in us, as a knife
Against which we may struggle! ocean girds
Unslackened the dry land, savannah-swards
Unweary sweep, – hills watch, unworn; and rife
Meek leaves drop yearly from the forest-trees,
To show above the unwasted stars that pass
In their old glory. O thou God of old,
Grant me some smaller grace than comes to these! –
But so much patience as a blade of grass
Grows by, contented through the heat and cold.

Elizabeth Barrett Browning

1806–61

Personal Reflections

Walking with God's approval

... we obey his commands and do what pleases him.
1 John 3:22

How much do you try to please other people? How important to you is it that you win the approval of your boss, your colleagues, your friends or your family? How much do other people's opinions matter to you?

Do you feel misunderstood? Are your good intentions misinterpreted? Your motives misconstrued? Do other people claim to know so much better than you what you are supposed to be doing and what your priorities should be? What are you going to do about it? Engage in lengthy explanations? Try to justify yourself? That would be a natural reaction. After all, we do not like to be misunderstood. We want people to think well of us.

But does it really matter what they think? Or, to rephrase the question and quote Paul: 'Am I now trying to win the approval of men, or of God?' (Gal. 1:10). If we are doing the will of God and trying to please Him, that is all that matters. True, it hurts when people attribute an ulterior motive to a genuinely loving action. But what a comfort it is to realise that God knows the motivation of your heart. The Bible tells us that it was because they lived by faith that 'our ancestors received approval' (Heb. 11:2, NRSV), God's approval, of course.

You cannot hold yourself responsible for other people's reactions. In Christ, we are *free* from the constraints and pressures of seeking the approval of others. We have a higher constraint, that of wanting to please our Master and gain His approval alone. This is the thought behind the above question put by Paul to the Galatian Christians.

This does not mean that we must not be sensitive to others. In some circumstances, we may very well be accountable to them. Correctly understood, Galatians 1:10 should not be seen as contradictory to the verse that says that, 'Each of us should please his neighbour for his good, to build him up' (Rom. 15:2), and to the verses that specify that 'the overseer must be above reproach' (1 Tim. 3:2a) and that 'Deacons … are to be men worthy of respect' (1 Tim. 3:8a).

We want to be accepted as we are, but do we accept others? Paul says, 'Therefore let us stop passing judgment on one another' (Rom. 14:13). Let us each concentrate on becoming the person that God wants us to be. It is enough to know that we are 'accepted in the beloved' (Eph. 1:6, AV).

Search me, O God, and know my heart;
test me and know my thoughts.
See if there is any wicked way in me,
and lead me in the way everlasting.
Psalm 139:23–24, NRSV

May the words of my mouth
and the meditation of my heart
be pleasing in your sight,
O Lord, my Rock and my Redeemer.
Psalm 19:14

God's approval

Misunderstood by those who hate
The Lamb that once was slain –
This kind of suffering makes one glad
And transforms all the pain.

But to be less than understood
By those one holds so dear,
By those who share one's life in Christ,
This causes many a tear.

So many things are misconstrued
And that does cause distress,
But look to Jesus and take heart:
He's ever quick to bless.

Submit to him the plans you make
And what you choose to do.
He knows the workings of your mind,
He'll keep your purpose true.

Lord, You who were despised and rejected, who were unfairly accused and humiliated, who were put to death unjustly in the most shameful way, You understand how we feel when we suffer injustices in this life, when we are falsely accused or simply misunderstood. Help us to react in love and humility. Thank You that You know us through and through. You know the motivations of our hearts. Thank You that we can leave matters in Your hands.

Personal Reflections

Walking through the valley

Even though I walk through the valley of the shadow of death,
I will fear no evil, for you are with me; your rod and your
staff, they comfort me.
Psalm 23:4

I n the unbearably hot European summer of 2003, my husband had the good idea of leaving the dry, stifling valley behind and driving up to the mountains and crossing three of the highest mountain passes in Switzerland, the Grimsel, the Furka and the Susten. How lovely it was, in that majestic environment, to breathe the cooler air and to see refreshing mountain streams cascading over the rocks!

But eventually we had to come back down to the valley again. We'd all like to stay on the mountaintop, but most of our life has to be lived out in the valley. The valley can symbolise both the humdrum routine of life and also sorrow and even death. It is not for nothing that a certain very hot valley in the United States is called 'Death Valley'!

In the New Testament, we read that '… Jesus took with him Peter, James and John … and led them up a high mountain by themselves' (Matt. 17:1). Up on that mountaintop Jesus 'was transfigured before them' (v.2). Then two Old Testament characters, Moses and Elijah, appeared and talked to Jesus. Peter, as impetuous as ever, wanted to build three shelters, so that they could all stay up there.

But Jesus had different plans. Later in the account (v.9), we read 'As they were coming down the mountain …' They could not stay up there on the mountaintop; they had to come back down into the valley and get on with life down here as before.

As we walk through the valleys of life, we can count on God's presence with us, to guide us, to sustain us and to comfort us. And that makes all the difference. He is in control:

You set the earth on its foundations,
so that it shall never be shaken.
You cover it with the deep as with a garment;
the waters stood above the mountains.
At your rebuke they flee;
at the sound of your thunder they take to flight;
They rose up to the mountains,
ran down to the valleys
to the place that you appointed for them.
You set a boundary that they may not pass,
so that they might not again cover the earth.
Psalm 104:5–9, NRSV

I will make rivers flow on barren heights,
and springs within the valleys.
Isaiah 41:18a

In the valley

And life goes on ... but to what end?
I wake to face another day.
I wash, I dress, I comb my hair,
I cook and eat, but cannot pray.
Nothing is real, except the pit
Of misery where I now sit.

I do not want to have to wake.
I do not want to face the day.
God, are you there? Don't hide your face.
Speak to me now. Show me your way.
Don't leave me in this grey despair.
Lift me up, Lord. Please hear my prayer.

Why, O God, did it have to be?
Just trust me, child. I'm in control.
Just walk by faith and not by sight.
One day you'll see what is the goal.
My purposes will be revealed,
And hurts and wounds will all be healed.

Think of my Word. What does it say?
I'll never leave you. You belong
To me, my child. You are my own.
Your grasp is weak, but mine is strong.
Though all is dark, I'll hold you fast.
Rest in my love; give me what's past.

I'll comfort you when faith grows frail.
I'll wipe the tears that dim your sight.
I'll lead you on until that day
When death and darkness change to light.
No mourning then, no more of pain
Because of him, the Lamb once slain.

Yes, Lord, how wonderful it is that we can count on Your presence even in the valley. Even as we go through the darkest hours of our lives, You are there at our side. You will never leave us. You bring strength and comfort and hope. Thank You.

Down in the valley with my Saviour I would go,
Where the flowers are blooming and the sweet waters flow;
Everywhere he leads me I would follow, follow on;
Walking in his footsteps till the crown be won.

Down in the valley with my Saviour I would go,
Where the storms are sweeping and the dark waters flow;
With his hand to lead me I will never, never fear;
Danger cannot harm me if my Lord is near.

Down in the valley or upon the mountain steep,
Close beside my Saviour would my soul ever keep;
He will lead me safely in the path that he has trod,
Up to where they gather on the hills of God.

William O. Cushing
1823–1903

Personal Reflections

Walking decently

… women should dress themselves modestly and decently in suitable
clothing, not with their hair braided, or with gold, pearls,
or expensive clothes, but with good works
1 Timothy 2:9–10, NRSV

W
e only need to see the latest women's fashions on TV to realise
that modesty and decency are not exactly the main criteria in
the designers' new styles! Seduction, more likely.

In Ephesus at the time that Paul wrote to Timothy, prostitutes,
immodestly and indecently clad, with overabundant jewellery and
exaggerated, extravagant hairstyles, would have abounded in the temple of
the goddess Diana.

Christian women were to be different. Their modest attire and simple
hairstyles would contrast with those of the pagan women. This does not
mean they were to be dowdy and unattractive. They were to be suitably
dressed, as befitting a follower of Christ.

What constitutes 'suitable clothing' must, I believe, be evaluated
culturally. These same principles of modesty and decency, applied in
our cultural setting, remain valid for us today. For many years I was
part of a church which attracts people from many nations. It truly is an
international church. The multicultural aspect of the church is reflected in
the dress of its members, both men and women. Brightly coloured saris,
braided African hairstyles or elaborate head coverings, beads and bangles,
embroidered shirts, shorts, all have their place amid the more sober garb
of their European and North American counterparts. Surely what Paul

means is that we should dress in a way that is culturally acceptable for a contemporary Christian.

Actually, in all that he says, what comes through as being more important than dress is Christian character. 'Good works' are more important than the clothes we wear, but our clothing and outward appearance and adornment should in no way be a stumbling-block to others (see 1 Cor. 8:9ff.) or incompatible with our professed reverence for God. This should be reflected in the way we dress, in the way we act, in the way we live.

'… as God's chosen people … clothe yourselves with compassion, kindness, humility, gentleness and patience' wrote Paul (Col. 3:12). Jesus said, '… let your light shine before men, that they may see your good deeds and praise your Father in heaven' (Matt. 5:16). And Peter echoed Jesus' words when he said, 'Live such good lives among the pagans that, though they accuse you of doing wrong, they may see your good deeds and glorify God …' (1 Pet. 2:12).

… all things should be done decently and in order.
1 Corinthians 14:40, NRSV

Lord, I want to live in a way that is pleasing to You. I want to walk decently. I pray that this may be reflected in the way I dress, in the way I act, in the way I relate to others, in the way I do my work. May every part of my life bring glory to You.

I will rejoice greatly in the LORD,
My soul will exult in my God;
For He has clothed me with garments of salvation,
He has wrapped me with a robe of righteousness,
As a bridegroom decks himself with a garland,
And as a bride adorns herself with her jewels.

Isaiah 61:10, NASB

Command those who are rich in the things of this life not to
be proud, but to place their hope, not in such an uncertain thing
as riches, but in God, who generously gives us everything for our
enjoyment. Command them to do good, to be rich in good works,
to be generous and ready to share with others. In this way they
will store up for themselves a treasure which will be a solid
foundation for the future. And then they will be able to win
the life which is true life.

1 Timothy 6:17–19, GNB

Personal Reflections

Walking in ancient paths

This is what the LORD says: 'Stand at the crossroads and look;
ask for the ancient paths, ask where the good way is, and walk in it,
and you will find rest for your souls.'
Jeremiah 6:16

Summer is a time when many people like to go on holiday, to have a change, to rest and relax. With this kind of a break in routine, it is very easy to temporarily lose the habit of walking with God each day. Regular Bible reading and prayer can easily get pushed out, as the rhythm of our life is different from usual.

Physical rest is good and necessary. We read that the prophet Elijah, stressed and tired and depressed, sat down under a broom tree '… and prayed that he might die …' (1 Kings 19:4). Then, after telling God how he felt '… he lay down under the tree and fell asleep' (v.5a). The rest and sleep did him good. Then, after eating some food brought to him by an angel, he '… lay down again' (v.6). The angel came again with more food, after which Elijah felt strong enough to embark upon the next stage of his journey.

If physical rest is beneficial for us, so is rest for our souls. And it is only as we draw close to God, through reading His Word and through prayer, that we can know this peace and rest that He longs to give us. Life is generally pretty stressful. Many of us are facing situations that are far from easy. We worry and fret. Anxiety gnaws at us.

Change is very rapid in today's world. We can easily become disorientated. Ancient landmarks seem to have disappeared. People are like travellers in a strange land, confronted by a variety of paths and not knowing which direction to take. Which way should we turn? Which path should we follow?

Are you at a crossroads in life, not knowing which way to go? Why not do as Jeremiah suggests in the above verse? Stand and look, rather than heedlessly do what everyone else is doing, or rush headlong into multiple activities without sober reflection. Stop and think. Exercise judgment. Evaluate. Seek 'the good way' and walk in it.

Jeremiah was basically telling God's people not to forsake the God of their fathers or the long-standing practices and traditions based on his word. 'Do not move an ancient boundary stone set up by your forefathers' (Prov. 22:28).

We have all at one time or another lost our way or required directions in order to find any given destination. The best way is to ask someone who knows. Jeremiah, too, says, 'Ask' – '… ask for the ancient paths'. If you realise that you have wandered far from God, it is not too late to turn round, to come back and walk again in the 'good way'. It is there that you will find deep peace and rest of heart and mind.

[You will] guide our feet into the path of peace.
Luke 1:79b

Make me to know your ways, O Lord;
teach me your paths.
Lead me in your truth, and teach me,
for you are the God of my salvation;
for you I wait all day long.
Be mindful of your mercy, O Lord, and of your steadfast love,
for they have been from of old.
Psalm 25:4–6, NRSV

The Lord's Prayer
(Matthew 6:9–13, NRSV)

Our Father

We have an intimate relationship with God. He is our Father and He loves us.

in heaven,

He reigns on high. He is sovereign.

hallowed be your name.

You are holy, completely 'other'.

Your kingdom come.

May everyone and everything on this earth bow down to You, worship You and submit to You. Reign 'down here', Lord, as well as 'up there'.

Your will be done,

Have Your own way, Lord. May all Your purposes be worked out and find fulfilment

on earth as it is in heaven.

here on earth, just like in heaven.

Give us this day our daily bread.

Please supply our material needs today (and every day). Thank You for home and family, for friends, for food and clothing. Thank You for Your beautiful world; for sun and warmth; for rain and trees and flowers; for rivers and seas and mountains; for birds and animals.

And forgive us our debts,

We need Your forgiveness, Lord, because we are sinful.

as we also have forgiven our debtors.

How could we not forgive others when You have forgiven us so much?

And do not bring us to the time of trial,

Help us to stand firm, Lord, and keep us from sinning. Don't let us get into situations where we may be tempted to sin.

but rescue us from the evil one.

Yes, Lord, keep us out of the devil's clutches.

Yes, Lord, teach me Your ways, so that I might walk in Your paths. I know that Your way is best. Keep me from wandering from the pathway.

Personal Reflections

Walking with thanksgiving

Give thanks to the LORD, for he is good; his love endures for ever.
Psalm 107:1

As we come to the last week of our summer readings, we want to end on a thankful note. No matter what tragedies may strike us, no matter what sorrows may engulf us, we always have reason to give thanks to God. We thank Him first of all for our Saviour and for 'every spiritual blessing' (see Eph. 1:3) that we have in Him: all those 'benefits' listed in Psalm 103 – His forgiveness, His love, His grace, His mercy, His compassion, His presence, His strength. And these are the things that matter, for these are eternal things that no one can take away. They will last forever.

We thank Him too for family and friends, for health, for food and clothing, for the roof over our heads, for the beauty of creation. Paul wrote to Timothy that God 'richly provides us with everything for our enjoyment' (1 Tim. 6:17b).

When things are going well we often hear people say, 'God is good'. But what about when things are not going quite so well? Is God still good? Our concept of things is partial and dim. God sees the whole picture. Sometimes He may permit trials and difficulties to bring us to repentance or to strengthen our faith. We may not perceive this to be 'goodness' at the time, and we may not feel very thankful, but God is looking ahead to the finished product. He is looking to our highest, ultimate good, rather than our passing pleasure. His goodness is not dependent on our subjective appraisal of it. Goodness is part of His character, one of His attributes.

A friend of mine, who has known much suffering and bereavement in her life, wrote to inform me of the death of her 'beloved friend'. In her grief, she concluded her letter with these words: 'God is good. This is still my testimony.' Another friend, diagnosed with terminal cancer, ended her message to us with the words: 'God is good'. The mother of a young boy with brain damage and many other serious bodily injuries due to a bad road accident, while in deep distress at her son's condition, also affirmed that 'the Lord is good'.

God's goodness is expressed through deeds – *good deeds* – or actions. And the psalm quoted opposite, Psalm 107, brings to our notice some of these expressions of God's goodness. It is addressed first and foremost to God's people Israel. Written in the context of Israel's history, it refers primarily to Israel's deliverance from Exile.

God has 'redeemed' His people (v.2) – bought them back from the enemy – and 'gathered' them to Himself (v.3). And that really is something to give thanks for! Peter tells us that we too have been redeemed – bought back – '… with the precious blood of Christ' (1 Pet. 1:19a). Let us, too, give thanks.

The verse quoted above mentions God's love, which 'endures for ever'. Love must be demonstrated. What is the highest, fullest expression of God's love to us? Paul wrote to the Christians in Rome: 'God demonstrates his own love for us in this: While we were still sinners, Christ died for us' (Rom. 5:8). While we were still sinners – totally undeserving of His love – Christ died for us. What a cause for thanksgiving!

I will praise God's name in song and glorify him with thanksgiving.
Psalm 69:30

Thank You, Lord, for Your great love to me. Thank You for demonstrating this love through dying in my place. Thank You for taking upon Yourself the punishment that I deserve. Thank You for paying the price. Thank You for the many blessings that You shower upon me. Thank You, too, that I can look forward to spending eternity in Your presence.

My God, I thank Thee, who hast made the earth so bright,
So full of splendor and of joy, beauty and light;
So many glorious things are here, noble and right.

I thank Thee, too, that Thou hast made joy to abound,
So many gentle thoughts and deeds circling us round,
That in the darkest spot of earth some love is found.

I thank Thee more, that all our joy is touched with pain,
That shadows fall on brightest hours, that thorns remain;
So that earth's bliss may be our guide, and not our chain.

For Thou, who knowest, Lord, how soon our weak heart clings,
Hast given us joys, tender and true, yet all with wings,
So that we see, gleaming on high, diviner things.

I thank Thee, Lord, that Thou hast kept the best in store:
We have enough, but not too much to long for more –
A yearning for a deeper peace not known before.

I thank Thee, Lord, that here our souls, though amply blest,
Can never find, although they seek, a perfect rest,
Nor ever shall, until they lean on Jesus' breast.

Anne Adelaide Procter
1825–64

Personal Reflections

Autumn

We continue walking with God each day into the 'season of mists and mellow fruitfulness',[1] when grapes are ripe on the vine and rustling leaves, yellow, russet and brown, are shuffled underfoot. Deep red Virginia Creeper glows on old grey stone walls in the golden evening sunlight.

One year we were able to admire the autumn colours in New England. We travelled from Delaware to visit a friend in Maine. With her we drove up to a ski resort in New Hampshire. Never had we seen such luminous tints!

This is the season when fruit comes to maturity, when farmers harvest their crops and store the abundance of their produce for the winter. There is a feeling of contentment and fulfilment:

> The LORD your God is bringing you into a fertile land – a land that has rivers and springs, and underground streams gushing out into the valleys and hills; a land that produces wheat and barley, grapes, figs, pomegranates, olives, and honey. There you will never go hungry or ever be in need.
>
> Deuteronomy 8:7–9a, GNB

These themes are picked up in some of the following meditations. We want to enter fully into all that the Lord has for us and learn to be content. Even if we have to walk through trials, these can have a positive result in our lives.

> *Blessed are those whose strength is in you,*
> *who have set their hearts on pilgrimage.*
> *As they pass through the Valley of Baca,*
> *they make it a place of springs;*
> *the autumn rains also cover it with pools.*
> *They go from strength to strength,*
> *till each appears before God in Zion.*
> Psalm 84:5–7

1. John Keats, *Ode to Autumn* (1795–1821).

Walking in freedom

*Live as free men, but do not use your freedom as
a cover-up for evil; live as servants of God.*

1 Peter 2:16

I once read a magazine article about a young Englishman in detention in Sri Lanka. While there he came to know the Lord as his Saviour. Even though he died in chains in that prison in 1999, he had found true freedom in Christ.

Many people are in prisons of their own making. The walls of Fremantle Prison in Western Australia imprisoned the British convicts who built them in the nineteenth century. We can be imprisoned by sin, by a dependency, by an addiction, by a relationship. But Jesus can break our chains and set us free.

> To the Jews who had believed in him, Jesus said, 'If you hold to my teaching, you are really my disciples. Then you will know the truth, and the truth will set you free.' They answered him, 'We are Abraham's descendants and have never been slaves of anyone. How can you say that we shall be set free?'
>
> Jesus replied, 'I tell you the truth, everyone who sins is a slave to sin. Now a slave has no permanent place in the family, but a son belongs to it for ever. So if the Son sets you free, you will be free indeed.'
>
> John 8:31–36

Just as a fish is in its element in water, so we are in our 'element' in our relationship with God, because that is what God intended from the beginning. He created us to be in relationship with Himself. This relationship was severed because of our sin, but in Christ we are brought back – in fact we are *bought* back, as Jesus paid the price for our sin – into fellowship with Him again.

So what in fact is true freedom in Jesus? It is the freedom to become the people God intended us to be, so that His purposes will be fulfilled in our lives, and so that He will be glorified. It is not licence to do whatever we like. That would very quickly lead to slavery again. Paul wrote to the Galatians: 'It is for freedom that Christ has set us free. Stand firm, then, and do not let yourselves be burdened again by a yoke of slavery' (Gal. 5:1).

To the Christians in Rome he wrote words that may seem paradoxical to us on a first reading: 'You have been set free from sin and have become slaves to righteousness. ... But now that you have been set free from sin and have become slaves to God, the benefit you reap leads to holiness, and the result is eternal life' (Rom. 6:18,22). We see that being 'slaves to God' is in fact true freedom and will lead to total fulfilment.

> *... Christ has set us free!*
> Galatians 5:1, GNB

Thank You, Lord, for the freedom that is mine in Christ. Please make me the person you want me to be. I am glad to be Your slave, because I know that You love me and that You want the best for me. I want to live in a way that brings glory to You.

Freedom

Imprisoned by secular freedom:
Smoke, drink, drugs, sex –
Anything goes.
'Eat, drink and be merry
For tomorrow we die'.

Lost, dead, far from their Maker.
No meaning to life.
Alienated, isolated –
Unshackled existence
Binding the young.

Liberated by One who enslaves them,
Taken captive so they might be free.
No longer autonomous –
Bought with a price.
Dead to self – and yet truly alive.

Personal Reflections

Walking carefully

There is a way that seems right to a man,
but in the end it leads to death.
Proverbs 14:12

When I was a child in Africa, I loved to ride my bike through the bush. But I had to be careful in case there were snakes on the path. What started out as a pleasurable activity could have ended in catastrophe if I had not been on my guard.

How tempting and enticing and attractive and alluring the world's pleasures can seem, especially to young people who have not yet 'tasted' much of what life can offer. And how short-sighted are they who get caught up in these pleasures. The world would have us live in the present, with no thought for the future. Jesus' parable of *The Rich Fool* should serve to put us on our guard:

> 'There was once a rich man who had land which bore good crops. He began to think to himself, "I haven't anywhere to keep all my crops. What can I do? This is what I will do," he told himself; "I will tear down my barns and build bigger ones, where I will store my corn and all my other goods. Then I will say to myself, Lucky man! You have all the good things you need for many years. Take life easy, eat, drink and enjoy yourself!" But God said to him, "You fool! This very night you will have to give up your life; then who will get all these things you have kept for yourself?"'
>
> And Jesus concluded, 'This is how it is with those who pile up riches for themselves but are not rich in God's sight.'
>
> Luke 12:16b–21, GNB

We need to choose our 'way' carefully, taking into account all the consequences of our decision, as did Moses, who 'chose to be ill-treated along with the people of God rather than to enjoy the pleasures of sin for a short time. He regarded disgrace for the sake of Christ as of greater value than the treasures of Egypt, because he was looking ahead to his reward' (Heb. 11:25–26).

Moses was not just considering this life. He was looking ahead to eternity. Why turn our back on Jesus' offer of life to the full, life in abundance, eternal life, in favour of a cheap imitation, which in fact is not life at all, but death?

> *You have made known to me the*
> *path of life;*
> *you will fill me with joy in your*
> *presence,*
> *with eternal pleasures at your*
> *right hand.*
> Psalm 16:11

Walking carefully

So much of pain is self-inflicted,
So much of woe is from my hand.
How can I then expect his comfort?
Or on his promises to stand?

Yet, God is gracious to forgive me
And consolation to me bring.
His mercy is for everlasting,
His love does cause my heart to sing.

But help me, Lord, not to court trouble,
And keep me in your perfect peace.
Give me the mind of Christ my Saviour,
Him to exalt, self to decrease.

Lord, keep me walking in Your ways. Thank You for your forgiveness and restoration at times when I have gone astray. Give me the right perspective, Lord, so that I will not become too attached to the things of this world. Help me, like Moses, to look ahead and not be sidetracked into the pleasures of this world.

He must increase, but I must decrease.
John 3:30, RSV

Personal Reflections

Walking fruitfully

*[Jesus said:] '... I chose you and appointed you to go
and bear fruit – fruit that will last. ...'*
John 15:16

T he theme of the study sessions at a ski weekend for the youth of our
church was, 'What would Jesus do?' Many of the young people were
sporting leather bracelets inscribed with the letters WWJD?.
What would Jesus do? Good question! Well, is it? Is it the question
we should be asking? Now, far be it from me to want to discourage any
young person – or older person – from doing what Jesus would do! But I
do wonder if, in asking this question, we are not putting the cart before the
horse. I mean, how can we do what Jesus would do if we are not like Jesus to
begin with? Surely the question we should be asking is not so much, 'What
would Jesus do?' but 'What is Jesus like?'

I need to become like Jesus in order to do what Jesus would do. That is
what God aims to do in my life – make me like Jesus. Jesus became like us
(God sent 'his own Son *in the likeness of sinful man* to be a sin offering. ...'
– Rom. 8:3b, my italics), so that we might become like Him ('... those God
foreknew he also predestined *to be conformed to the likeness of his Son* ...'
– Rom. 8:29, my italics).

This is only possible as we are indwelt by Him and as the Holy Spirit
does His transforming work within us. '... Christ lives in me ...' affirmed
Paul (Gal. 2:20). Later, in the same letter, he wrote: '... the fruit of the Spirit
is love, joy, peace, patience, kindness, goodness, faithfulness, gentleness and
self-control' (5:22–23a). It is only as Jesus takes control of our lives that we
will reflect Him in the way we live. It is only as we 'remain' in Him and He

remains in us that we will 'bear much fruit' (John 15:5).

When Jesus said in His Sermon on the Mount, 'You have heard that it was said … But I tell you …' (Matt. 5:21–48), He was not just replacing one set of rules with another. There is no way we can do as Jesus would do in our own strength. It would amount to legalism and we would inevitably fall short. It would be a slavish imitation, rather than fruit-bearing from a heart of love. '… God has poured out his love into our hearts by the Holy Spirit, whom he has given us' wrote Paul to the Romans (5:5).

We must be more concerned about 'being' than 'doing'. The actions will then follow as a reflection and outpouring of God's life within us. 'The imitation of Christ' is all very well. But who wants to be content with an imitation? Surely the real thing – the authentic product – is of more value. You might say, 'Well, it will all work out the same in the end. Being like Jesus will enable me to do what Jesus would do.' Certainly, but if our emphasis is wrong to start with, our 'doing' will be little more than human effort devoid of God's power and that essential ingredient, love.

And it is my prayer that your love may abound more and more,
with knowledge and all discernment, so that you may approve what
is excellent, and may be pure and blameless for the day of Christ,
filled with the fruits of righteousness which come through Jesus
Christ, to the glory and praise of God.
Philippians 1:9–11, RSV

Jesus said:

> 'I am the true vine, and My Father is the vinedresser. Every branch
> in Me that does not bear fruit, He takes away; and every branch
> that bears fruit, He prunes it so that it may bear more fruit. You are
> already clean because of the word which I have spoken to you. Abide
> in Me, and I in you. As the branch cannot bear fruit of itself unless
> it abides in the vine, so neither can you unless you abide in Me.
>
> 'I am the vine, you are the branches; he who abides in Me, and I
> in him, he bears much fruit, for apart from Me you can do nothing.
> If anyone does not abide in Me, he is thrown away as a branch and
> dries up; and they gather them, and cast them into the fire and they
> are burned. If you abide in Me, and My words abide in you, ask
> whatever you wish, and it will be done for you. My Father is glorified
> by this, that you bear much fruit, and so prove to be My disciples.'
>
> John 15:1–8, NASB

**Thank You, Lord, for living in me. Help me to remain united to You, so
that I will bear fruit to Your glory. Transform me, Lord. Make me like
Jesus, so that the fruit of the Spirit will be evident in my life.**

Personal Reflections

Walking with compassion

… be compassionate and humble.
1 Peter 3:8

What are some of the causes of fear in our world today? Not in any particular order of priority, we could mention unemployment, AIDS, terrorism, famine, floods, earthquakes, pollution … Every day on the news we see the ravages caused by wars that are raging in many parts of the globe. The spotlight swings from Iraq to Palestine, to Haiti to the Ivory Coast … Other causes of anxiety would be old age, illness and finally, the last enemy, death.

Of course when things are going well (for us), it is relatively easy to close our eyes and pretend that these problems do not exist. After all, they are not happening to me – yet. And why should they? Rather, why shouldn't they? It is so easy for us to opt out of the real world. After all, Christians aren't supposed to be anxious, are they? But is the peace we claim to possess any more than indifference? Is the trust we profess to have, anything more than illusion? Are we acting as responsible human beings? Or are we behaving like ostriches?

In such a dilemma we could legitimately ask ourselves, 'What would Jesus do?' Well, what would He do? How many times in the Gospels do we read of Jesus having compassion, or being 'moved with' or 'filled with' compassion? To have compassion means to suffer with … How then can we who profess to be followers of Christ remain indifferent to the sufferings of those around us? Paul urged the Christians in Rome to 'mourn [or weep] with those who mourn' (Rom. 12:15b).

The compassion Jesus felt drove Him to action, as in the case of the leper who begged Him, 'If you are willing, you can make me clean.' The narrative continues: 'Filled with compassion, Jesus reached out his hand and touched the man. ... Immediately the leprosy left him and he was cured' (Mark 1:40–42).

Similarly, faced with the large crowd of over 5,000 people, Jesus '... had compassion on them and healed their sick' (Matt. 14:14b). Then He fed them. When He went to the town of Nain, He saw a widow weeping because her son had died. We read, 'When the Lord saw her, his heart went out to her and he said, "Don't cry".' (Luke 7:13). Then He brought the young man back from the dead and 'gave him back to his mother' (v.15b).

The needs we see around us should at least drive us to our knees in prayer. This is what Jesus exhorted His disciples to do in Matthew 9:36–38: 'When he saw the crowds, he had compassion on them, because they were harassed and helpless, like sheep without a shepherd. Then he said to his disciples, "The harvest is plentiful but the workers are few. Ask the Lord of the harvest, therefore, to send out workers into his harvest field."' May we, too, pray with compassion and then act with compassion.

The Lord is gracious and compassionate,
slow to anger and rich in love.
Psalm 145:8

Jesus said:

'When the Son of Man comes as King and all the angels with him, he will sit on his royal throne, and the people of all the nations will be gathered before him. Then he will divide them into two groups, just as a shepherd separates the sheep from the goats. He will put the righteous people on his right and the others on his left. Then the King will say to the people on his right, "Come, you that are blessed by my Father! Come and possess the kingdom which has been prepared for you ever since the creation of the world. I was hungry and you fed me, thirsty and you gave me a drink; I was a stranger and you received me in your homes, naked and you clothed me; I was sick and you took care of me, in prison and you visited me."

'The righteous will then answer him, "When, Lord, did we ever see you hungry and feed you, or thirsty and give you a drink? When did we ever see you a stranger and welcome you in our homes, or naked and clothe you? When did we ever see you sick or in prison, and visit you?" The King will reply, "I tell you, whenever you did this for one of the least important of these brothers of mine, you did it for me!"

'Then he will say to those on his left, "Away from me, you that are under God's curse! Away to the eternal fire which has been prepared for the Devil and his angels! I was hungry but you would not feed me, thirsty but you would not give me a drink; I was a stranger but you would not welcome me in your homes, naked but you would not clothe me; I was sick and in prison but you would not take care of me."

'Then they will answer him, "When, Lord, did we ever see you hungry or thirsty or a stranger or naked or sick or in prison, and would not help you?" The King will reply, "I tell you, whenever you refused to help one of these least important ones, you refused to help me." These, then, will be sent off to eternal punishment, but the righteous will go to eternal life.'

Matthew 25:31–46, GNB

Dear Lord, help me to remember the teaching of Your Word. Enable me to put it into practice. I pray for those who are living in fear of terrorist attacks or war. I pray for those who are ill or homeless or dying. I pray for the unemployed and for those who are hungry. I pray for world leaders – those in authority – that they may govern fairly and wisely. May I have compassion on those in need whom You place on my path.

Personal Reflections

Walking in abundance

'Whoever has will be given more, and he will have an abundance.'
Matthew 13:12a

When our children were young, we spent some happy family holidays on a farm in Somerset. Although our family was living at a relaxed pace for that short time, we were conscious that all around us work was going on as usual. And farmers work hard! They spend long hours in the fields, ploughing, sowing, and later tending their crops, often in adverse weather conditions (in England at any rate!). When autumn comes, the farmer deserves the abundant harvest that follows such devoted toil.

Just as the farmer works hard, and sometimes faces difficulties, so we all go through times of discouragement, often because of our circumstances. How do we handle these negative feelings? By focusing on the circumstances and falling into self-pity? Or by doing what the psalmist did in Psalms 42 and 43? He engaged in a healthy examination of himself (as distinct from unhealthy introspection!) and his situation, which led him to hope in God.

> Why are you downcast, O my soul?
>   Why so disturbed within me?
> Put your hope in God …
>   Psalm 42:5,11; 43:5

Through the mouth of His prophet, God said, 'I will heal my people and will let them enjoy abundant peace and security' (Jer. 33:6). Addressing ourselves through the words of Scripture or through the words of a hymn can lift us up and make us focus on the Lord:

> O soul are you weary and troubled?
> No light in the darkness you see?
> There's light for a look at the Saviour,
> And life more abundant and free.
>
> Turn your eyes upon Jesus,
> Look full in his wonderful face,
> And the things of earth will grow strangely dim
> In the light of his glory and grace.[2]

True, our situation may be difficult, but how much does Jesus mean to us? 'Life more abundant and free' is ours in Christ, no matter what the circumstances. We are more alive (in Him) than the richest, most active, pleasure-loving people in the world … who remain dead in their sins. Why are we so easily blinded to this truth? Why are we so often content to live in spiritual poverty? Why are our circumstances more real to us than the love of the Saviour?

Paul wrote to the Romans: 'If, because of one man's trespass, death reigned through that one man, how much more will those who receive the abundance of grace and the free gift of righteousness reign in life through the one man, Jesus Christ' (Rom. 5:17, RSV).

Let us walk in the abundance of all that He gives us. Jesus said: 'I came that they may have life, and have it abundantly' (John 10:10b, NRSV). He stepped into this world in order to bring life. Real life. Eternal life. Abundant life.

> *The grace of our Lord was poured out on me abundantly,*
> *along with the faith and love that are in Christ Jesus.*
> 1 Timothy 1:14

2. Helen H. Lemmell, Singspiration Music/Brentwood Benson Music Publishing, 1922.

Thank You, Lord, for the abundant life You have given me. I want to walk in the abundance of all the riches that are mine in Christ. And I pray that all the glory will be Yours.

As we reflect on the deserving farmer enjoying the abundant harvest after his hard work in the fields, Psalm 65 tells us how God Himself looks after the land, which yields rich fruit in abundance:

> *You care for the land and water it;*
> *you enrich it abundantly.*
> *The streams of God are filled with water*
> *to provide the people with corn,*
> *for so you have ordained it.*
> *You drench its furrows*
> *and level its ridges;*
> *You soften it with showers*
> *and bless its crops.*
> *You crown the year with your bounty,*
> *and your carts overflow with abundance.*
> verses 9–11

Personal Reflections

Walking through the daily grind

Serve wholeheartedly, as if you were serving the Lord, not men.
Ephesians 6:7

I n a radio interview I had about my book *Seeking God's Face*,[3] the interviewer asked several questions about the book and about my relationship with God. Then, in an attempt to come back down to earth, she asked me about the chores of daily life. She wanted me to convey to her listeners that I did have a 'normal' life, that I did occupy myself with housework and shopping and cooking and washing and ironing …

Her question was, 'Is there a life without Jesus?' I think she expected an affirmative answer. Some people may tend to compartmentalise their lives, but as far as I am concerned, there is no 'life without Jesus'. One of the wonderful aspects of being in relationship with Him is that His presence pervades every part of my life, including the most mundane tasks. I consciously want to bring Jesus in to everything that I do and everything that I am involved in.

I made a reference to Brother Lawrence in *Seeking God's Face*. Even though he did not at all like working in a monastery kitchen, Brother Lawrence's whole attitude was transformed when he realised that God was with him and that it was God whom he was serving.

The abundance we talked about last week is of course to be shared. 'Freely you have received, freely give' said Jesus to His disciples (Matt. 10:8). As I was meditating on this truth, and thinking about the different tasks that I accomplish each day, I handed all my household jobs over to the Lord, and they took on a new dimension.

3. Bible Reading Fellowship, 2004.

I had the privilege some years ago of spending a few days away alone in the Swiss Alps. While I was there, I walked for miles each day through woodland paths with breathtaking views, communing with the Lord and talking to Him about what constituted my daily routine at home. It was during that time that I wrote the following short prayers:

Lord,
Help me to see the glorious
In the mundane;
To realize that
When I'm serving others,
So am I serving you.

As I make this meal, Lord,
I offer up to you
This act of service and communion.
May our fellowship be sweet
Around the table,
As together with you
We share our bread.

As I do my washing, Lord,
I thank you for your cleansing blood
That washed me white as snow.
May my life reflect your purity
In all that I am,
All that I do.

As I do this ironing, Lord,
Iron out in me
Every crease and wrinkle,
All that marrs your image.
Make me more like you.

As I clean my house, Lord,
And make it a welcome place to be,
A place of rest and refuge,
Remove from me the dirt and dust
That cling so closely.
Cleanse me anew.

As I teach this lesson, Lord,
And share with others
The knowledge you have given me.
May I be humble and lowly
To learn of you.
Give me an open ear
And an obedient heart.

Sanctify these different tasks
As I do them all for you,
May I do them joyfully and well,
In an attitude of love and service.

*Whatever you do, work at it with all your heart, as working for the
Lord, not for men … It is the Lord Christ you are serving.*
Colossians 3:23–24

Personal Reflections

Walking to maturity

The righteous will flourish like a palm tree,
they will grow like a cedar of Lebanon.
Psalm 92:12

I still remember, as a child in Zambia, the day two new girls appeared in my class at school. These ten-year-old twins, Anne and Elizabeth, were soon counted among my best friends. It is thanks to them and their parents, who had come to Lusaka as missionaries that I came to understand that Jesus loved me enough to die for me. It was through this missionary family that I became a Christian. They were my spiritual parents, and I was their child in the faith.

In the same way, Paul had been instrumental in Timothy's conversion, and he addresses him at the beginning of his first letter, as 'my true son in the faith' (1 Tim. 1:2). Timothy's mother and grandmother were both godly women, who must have been influential in the life of the young Timothy. Paul writes to Timothy of his '… sincere faith, which first lived in your grandmother Lois and in your mother Eunice …' (2 Tim. 1:5).

However, the phrase 'my true son' would lead us to believe – and this fact is confirmed by other letters written by Paul – that not only did Timothy initially come to faith through Paul's ministry, but he also went on to grow spiritually, walking to maturity, by faithfully following his teaching and example.

Amar, from Sri Lanka, came into our church at age eleven, with his mother and younger sister, as a result of a tragic road accident involving the whole family in which his father was killed. Amar became a Christian at a young age and has gone on to greater understanding and deeper commitment as God has been at work in his life. As a young adult, he took on responsibilities within the church and went on to study theology.

There are few things more encouraging to us as Christians than to see young people come to faith in Christ and grow to spiritual maturity and Christian leadership.

Since I became a Christian, many godly people have invested in my life and it is thanks to them and to my daily walk with God that I have grown in the faith. I continue to walk on to spiritual maturity. And yet, I confess that I am slow to learn, and the Lord has often had to teach me the same lessons over and over again. How patient He is!

Our physical bodies will not grow without food to nourish them. To become spiritually mature, we need regular spiritual food. We need to feed upon the Word of God continually. We need to keep close to the One who said, 'I am the bread of life' (John 6:35).

We ought always to thank God for you …
because your faith is growing more and more …
2 Thessalonians 1:3

Lord, may I, like Timothy, remain faithful to Your Word. May I grow spiritually. Thank You that You are the bread of life. I want to walk to maturity in You. Thank You that I am not alone. You are walking with me, and You have given me brothers and sisters to encourage me along the way.

O Jesus Christ, grow Thou in me,
And all things else recede:
My heart be daily nearer Thee,
From sin be daily freed.

Each day let Thy supporting might
My weakness still embrace;
My darkness vanish in Thy light,
Thy life my death efface.

In Thy bright beams which on me fall
Fade every evil thought;
That I am nothing, Thou art all,
I would be daily taught.

More of Thy glory let me see,
Thou Holy, Wise and True!
I would Thy living image be,
In joy and sorrow too.

Fill me with gladness from above,
Hold me by strength divine!
Lord, let the glow of Thy great love
Through my whole being shine.

Make this poor self grow less and less,
Be Thou my life and aim:
O make me daily, through Thy grace,
More meet to bear Thy name!

Johann Caspar Lavater 1741–1801
translated by Elizabeth Lee Smith 1817–98

*'I am the bread of life,' Jesus told them. 'Those who come to me will
never be hungry; those who believe in me will never be thirsty …
I am the living bread that came down from heaven. If anyone
eats this bread, he will live for ever. The bread that I will give him is
my flesh, which I give so that the world may live … Those who eat
my flesh and drink my blood have eternal life, and I will raise them
to life on the last day. For my flesh is the real food; my blood is the
real drink. Those who eat my flesh and drink my blood live in me,
and I live in them. The living Father sent me, and because of him
I live also. In the same way whoever eats me will live because of me.
This, then, is the bread that came down from heaven; it is not like
the bread that your ancestors ate. They later died, but those
who eat this bread will live for ever.'*
John 6:35,51,54–58, GNB

Personal Reflections

Walking in obedience

And this is love: that we walk in obedience to his commands.
2 John 6

My husband loves to watch the weather channel on TV! Particularly in the United States, with its vast variety of different climates and meteorological conditions, it does indeed make for fascinating, impressive viewing.

Noah, however, did not have this privilege. There was no meteorological office to forecast a deluge. Apparently there were no signs in the sky either to herald the oncoming flood. There was only God's word.

Noah is one example, found in the Old Testament, of implicit obedience. God spoke. Noah obeyed and acted. God's word was sufficient for him. God said, '… make yourself an ark' (Gen. 6:14). And when God had given him the dimensions, we read that 'Noah did everything just as God commanded him' (Gen. 6:22).

But who is Noah? The Bible tells us that 'Noah was a righteous man, blameless among the people of his time, and he *walked with God*' (Gen. 6:9, my italics). It also tells us that '… Noah found favour in the eyes of the LORD' (v.8).

Obeying God implies submitting to His will. Meditating on the events around the Easter story, I was suddenly struck forcibly by the fact that if Jesus, who was without sin, and who was one with the Father, had to say, '… not my will, but yours be done' (Luke 22:42), then how much more do I need to say it, sinful, wayward creature that I am.

We prefer to go our own way. We want our longings to be fulfilled. We desire instant gratification. Yielding to God's will, obeying Him, is too costly, too painful. And yet we know that ultimately God's way is best. So, if we do really want to obey Him and please Him and live for Him, then what a struggle goes on inside us, until we finally surrender and give in.

God spoke to the Israelites in the desert in this way: '… if you obey me fully … then out of all nations you will be my treasured possession' (Exod. 19:5a). Do you want to be God's 'treasured possession'? Then, submit to Him and obey Him like Noah did.

To walk with God and obey Him, to do God's work in God's way, using God's resources, should be our aim. We may tremble beneath the crushing load, but we can count on God's presence and strength. He will not let us down. He will enable us to bring to completion the work that He calls us to do. Our part is to step out in obedience and use the gifts that He has given us.

To obey is better than sacrifice …
1 Samuel 15:22b

Obedience

Full obedience, nothing less,
And only then the Lord will bless.
Just look to him and him alone.
Self sits no longer on the throne.
Open your hand and share your part.
The Lord commends a generous heart.

What wealth is ours from God's own store!
In Christ we lack not one thing more.
All things are ours, and his we are,
Redeemer, Saviour, Morning Star.

Lord, I know that Your way is best, but sometimes I find it hard to obey, especially when I don't understand or I can't see the outcome. Help me to trust You, Lord, in everything, and to obey You.

When we walk with the Lord
In the light of His Word,
What a glory He sheds on our way!
While we do His good will,
He abides with us still,
And with all who will trust and obey.

Trust and obey,
For there's no other way
To be happy in Jesus,
But to trust and obey.

John Henry Sammis
1846–1919

Personal Reflections

Walking to victory

... do not be afraid ... For the LORD your God is the one who goes with you to fight for you against your enemies to give you victory.
Deuteronomy 20:1,4

We only have to switch on our radio or television to hear of fighting, wars and killing. We all have battles to fight in life. We all have enemies. The Bible tells us that in the Christian life '... we are not fighting against human beings but against the wicked spiritual forces in the heavenly world' (Eph. 6:12, GNB). The kind of enemies that we face would prevent us from entering fully into all that the Lord has for us, from becoming all that we are potentially in Jesus Christ.

How do you react when you are up against difficult situations? It is so easy, and probably natural, to feel anxious, afraid, lacking in confidence. In chapter 20 of Deuteronomy, the people of Israel, about to enter the promised land, were confronted by enemies more powerful, more numerous and better equipped than they. Their enemies had horses and chariots, whereas the Israelites were almost certainly on foot. The enemy army was bigger too. It sounds as if there was not much hope for Israel.

The above words of encouragement from the book of Deuteronomy were given to the Israelites just before entering the promised land. They had reached the River Jordan and were about to cross over into Canaan, a land inhabited by many other nations.

A generation earlier, under the leadership of Moses, men had been sent to spy out the land and had brought back reports of very big strong people and large fortified towns. The terrified Israelites had refused to budge. They would have preferred to go back to Egypt rather than face the enemy. In spite of urging from Joshua and Caleb, there was no way they were going to take possession of that good land 'flowing with milk and honey' (Num. 14:8). So they had stayed in the desert and died there.

Now Moses is at the end of his life and the next generation of Israelites is preparing to cross the Jordan and face the enemy, this time under Joshua's leadership. Moses encourages them to count on the Lord's presence and to walk forward confidently. How easy it is to reason in such a way: 'I am weak, with few resources, so I will automatically fail.' But such reasoning does not take into account the presence and provision of the omnipotent God, who promised to give His people the victory.

The Israelites are told not to be afraid. This was no unrealistic pat on the back, offering ill-founded, hypothetical comfort – 'Don't worry. Everything will be all right.' This was real. They had a very good reason not to be afraid. Were they not God's own people? And had He not already done mighty works for them as He brought them out of Egypt and up to the promised land? Would He abandon them now that they were about to claim this land as their own? Of course not! They could count on His presence with them. Victory was assured!

Situations that we face, circumstances that we encounter, often cause us to tremble. Responsibility weighs heavily upon us. Enemies abound. Do we then remain static? Paralysed, are we incapable of moving forward? What are some of your enemies? There is the devil. The way to combat him is to 'Put on all the armour that God gives you, so that you will be able to stand up against the Devil's evil tricks' (Eph. 6:11, GNB). God has told us not to fear or be discouraged. He has promised to be with us. Not only will He be with us, but He will also fight for us. That does not mean that we remain passive. As we take up our positions, God will give us the victory. Then there are inward enemies: our sinful nature at war with our spiritual nature (see Gal. 5:17). And finally death – the 'last enemy to be destroyed' (1 Cor. 15:26).

Knowing that God has promised never to leave us gives us the courage that we need. Knowing that the Lord is by our side means that we can walk confidently through life, trusting Him to fulfil His purposes in us and through us. If you have put your trust in Jesus, then you too belong to God's own people. What mighty work has He done for you? He saved you from sin and from Satan's power. Jesus rose victorious from the grave. You share in His victory!

Do not be afraid or discouraged ... For the battle is not yours, but God's. ... You will not have to fight this battle. Take up your positions; stand firm and see the deliverance the LORD will give you ... the LORD will be with you.
2 Chronicles 20:15,17

Thank You, Lord, that in You we can have the victory. You have told us to resist the devil and he will flee from us. Thank You for the armour You have given us to enable us to be victorious and stand firm. Help me not to be afraid as I face spiritual battles. Help me to count on You for deliverance.

Finally, be strong in the Lord and in the strength of his power. Put on the whole armour of God, so that you may be able to stand against the wiles of the devil. ... Stand therefore, and fasten the belt of truth around your waist, and put on the breastplate of righteousness. As shoes for your feet put on whatever will make you ready to proclaim the gospel of peace. With all of these, take the shield of faith, with which you will be able to quench all the flaming arrows of the evil one. Take the helmet of salvation, and the sword of the Spirit, which is the word of God. Pray in the Spirit at all times ...
Ephesians 6:10–11,14–18, NRSV

Fierce may be the conflict,
Strong may be the foe,
But the king's own army
None can overthrow:
Round his standard ranging,
Victory is secure;
For his truth unchanging
Makes the triumph sure.
Joyfully enlisting,
By Thy grace divine,
We are on the Lord's side,
Saviour, we are Thine.

Frances Ridley Havergal
1836–79

Personal Reflections

Walking with contentment

But those who want to get rich fall into temptation and are caught
in the trap of many foolish and harmful desires, which pull them
down to ruin and destruction.
For the love of money is a source of all kinds of evil.
1 Timothy 6:9–10a, GNB

With a Singaporean friend, who was in our home for a meal, we talked about what it is that makes a person respected. Academic achievement? Noble birth? He was in no doubt at all that in Asia the criterion is wealth. If you are wealthy, you are respected. If you have riches, you are looked up to. Hence the love of money! Anyone who has ever been to Las Vegas will have been dazzled, not only by the lights, but also by the vast quantity of gaming machines in each casino and the incredible number of people – many of them older, lone women – gambling in a sort of frenetic desperation. My husband had a prison ministry in Geneva. Some of the men he came in contact with there were wealthy people … in prison for fraud. Some spoke of the emptiness inside. Material wealth brings no satisfaction, no contentment, no fulfilment. This God-shaped void (to paraphrase Blaise Pascal) can only be filled by God Himself.

'Keep your lives free from the love of money' writes the author of the letter to the Hebrews, 'and be content with what you have …' (13:5). Taken out of context, these words could seem like a command to instant contentment. This may not surprise us, though, as we are so used to having everything 'instant', from coffee to practically every kind of 'mix'. But God does not usually work that way. His transforming work is progressive – a process, often long.

We once had a wedding at our church at which five young girls called Jennifer were present! The bride's name was Jennifer, as was that of one of the bridesmaids. Some years before this happy event, Jennifer the bride had confided to one of the other Jennifers how much she wanted to find the man of her dreams and get married. The other Jennifer had pointed her to a verse in Psalm 37, which reads: 'Delight yourself in the LORD and he will give you the desires of your heart' (v.4). The Lord indeed graciously granted Jennifer's desire for a husband. At the wedding, this verse was printed on the order of service. The bride also requested that the sermon at the wedding service be based on that verse. When reading this psalm, it is very easy to pass straight to the second part of the verse: 'He will give you the desires of your heart.' We then conclude: 'Wow! That's great! God is going to give me everything I want!' Wait a minute. Is that what the verse really says? It is very easy for us to focus on our desires. But surely this verse is telling us that God is to be our focus. We have all that we need in Him.

Whether we realise it or not, I believe He is the object of our deepest desires. We may only be conscious of our felt needs and desires, and we may not realise that Jesus is the One – the only One – who can meet our deepest needs. Surely once we understand this, then our deepest desire will be to know Him better. It is only in Him that we will find true fulfilment and satisfaction and contentment. Paul wrote '... I have *learned* to be content whatever the circumstances. ... I have *learned* the secret of being content in any and every situation ...' (Phil. 4:11–12, my italics). This was no instant contentment, but the result of a learning process. Walking with contentment means submitting to God's will, trusting Him, and realising that we have all that we need in Him.

> *... godliness with contentment is great gain.*
> 1 Timothy 6:6

Contentment

Lord, give me a longing in my heart,
An ache, for you.
I ache so much for other things,
Some of them true
And good and honourable,
But not for you.

This restlessness, oh! where will it end?
In trust, in you.
What else can really satisfy,
My soul renew?
All else is chasing the wind.
True rest, in you.

Lord, still all the longings of my soul,
Except for you.
My yearning heart can know no peace
Unless you do.
I can have a quiet mind
Only in you.

Lord, I want to learn, like the apostle Paul, in every situation, whatever state I'm in, whatever my circumstances might be, to be content. Please teach me, Lord.

Contentment

He that is down needs fear no fall;
He that is low, no pride;
He that is humble, ever shall
Have God to be his guide.
I am content with what I have,
Little be it, or much:
And, Lord, contentment still I crave,
Because thou savest such.

John Bunyan
1628–88

Personal Reflections

Walking in wealth

The blessing of the LORD brings wealth …
Proverbs 10:22

Pearls were once considered to be the most precious things in the world.
Jesus told a story about them. He said: '… the kingdom of heaven is like
a merchant looking for fine pearls. When he found one of great value, he
went away and sold everything he had and bought it' (Matt. 13:45–46). Men
risked their lives in order to find pearls. The merchant in this story sold all
his possessions – not just his other pearls, which in themselves would have
been of inestimable value – in order to possess the one most valuable pearl.
He did this because he recognised the great worth and the intrinsic beauty
of that pearl.

Why do we hold onto things – maybe good things, precious things
– instead of letting them go for Jesus' sake? Is it because we have not yet
realized the incomparable value of the kingdom of heaven? The psalmist
says: '… Blessed is the man who fears the LORD. Wealth and riches are in his
house' (Psa. 112:1,3a).

This is something that Paul did realise. He counted all his human riches
and prestige as 'loss for the sake of Christ'. He added, 'What is more, I
consider everything a loss compared to the surpassing greatness of knowing
Christ Jesus my Lord' (Phil. 3:7–8).

True wealth is found only in Jesus. Paul wrote: 'For you know the
grace of our Lord Jesus Christ, that though he was rich, yet for your sakes
he became poor, so that you through his poverty might become rich'
(2 Cor. 8:9).

Jesus says to His disciples: 'Sell your possessions and give to the poor' (Luke 12:33). He tells them not to be afraid 'for your Father has been pleased to give you the kingdom' (Luke 12:32). If God gives us the kingdom, then surely we can give to those in need, as did the believers we read about in the book of Acts: 'Selling their possessions and goods, they gave to anyone as he had need' (2:45).

Jesus also said, 'Do not store up for yourselves treasures on earth, where moth and rust destroy, and where thieves break in and steal. But store up for yourselves treasures in heaven, where moth and rust do not destroy, and where thieves do not break in and steal. For where your treasure is, there your heart will be also' (Matt. 6:19–21).

Where is your treasure? What is the object of your thoughts, your affections, your desires? What or who has first place in your life?

And my God will meet all your needs
according to his glorious riches in Christ Jesus.
Philippians 4:19

Thank You, Lord, for promising to meet all my needs. Thank You that I have found 'treasures in heaven', treasures that will last and not be destroyed. I praise You that I have all that I need in You and that I can look forward to spending eternity with You.

Wealth

Lord, I want more.
More of yourself, your love, your life.
And a voice within whispering
That I must give
More of myself, my love, my life.
For he who loses his life
Will find it.
He who abases himself
Will be exalted.

And yet the longing remains
For something deeper.
The hunger's still there
For something higher.
Higher up and deeper in.
No longer standing on the edge.
Plunging into the depths;
Reaching up to the heights.

I talk of knowing you, Lord.
How can I know you whom
The heavens cannot contain?
And yet there's Jesus,
Equal with the Father,
Becoming poor so I might be rich.
And the longing still remains.
The thirst is not assuaged.

Blessed are those who hunger and thirst
for righteousness, for they shall be satisfied.
Matthew 5:6, NASB

The apostle Paul told the Christians in Colosse how much he was struggling for them and for the believers in Laodicea. He said:

> I do this in order that they may be filled with courage and may be drawn together in love, and so have the full wealth of assurance which true understanding brings. In this way they will know God's secret, which is Christ himself. He is the key that opens all the hidden treasures of God's wisdom and knowledge.
>
> Colossians 2:2–3, GNB

Personal Reflections

Walking through trials

Testing [or trials] will surely come.
Ezekiel 21:13

In Europe for his studies, Amjad became a believer in Jesus Christ and was baptised. He then returned to his country of Pakistan, where he knew his life could be in danger, living as a Christian in a Muslim society. He was anticipating walking through trials. I wonder what kind of reception you get when you try to tell people about Jesus. Hostility? Indifference? Mockery? Scorn? Interest? In many parts of the world Christians are persecuted for their faith. How do you think you would stand up to such trials?

We once had a visit in our church from Cynthia, a woman from Sri Lanka, who has done a tremendous work among children living in slum areas of Colombo. As she and her helpers taught the Christian faith to these little ones, they encountered much opposition. But they persevered in spite of the trials and have had the joy of seeing many children, as well as a number of their parents, come to a saving faith in Christ.

Throughout the worst of the war, our friends John and Nancy, with their two children, stayed in Lebanon where God has called them to reach young people with the gospel. As he avoided snipers on the streets of Beirut, John firmly believed that he and his family were safer there, in the centre of God's will in spite of their trials, than they would have been in any other place.

So often we pray that God will change our circumstances. We think, 'If only this particular situation were different …' or 'If only God would remove this difficulty or that' or 'If only I lived somewhere else' then I would feel so much better, and everything would be all right. Life without trials, how great that would be!

Peter gives us the right perspective. It is interesting how, at the beginning of his first letter, he talks almost in the same breath, as it were, about rejoicing and about trials. Yes, trials will come upon us, he says, and they will cause us grief: '… you may have had to suffer grief in all kinds of trials' (1 Pet. 1:6). But he explains that the trials that come upon us are meant to strengthen our faith. He says, 'These have come so that your faith – of greater worth than gold, which perishes even though refined by fire – may be proved genuine and may result in praise, glory and honour when Jesus Christ is revealed' (v.7). And he knows that we can look beyond our trials and 'greatly rejoice' in the 'inheritance that can never perish, spoil or fade – kept in heaven for [us]' (v.4). In fact a few chapters further on in his letter, he comes back to this same theme. He writes: 'Dear friends, do not be surprised at the painful trial you are suffering … But rejoice that you participate in the sufferings of Christ, so that you may be overjoyed when his glory is revealed' (1 Pet. 4:12–13).

Writing to the Corinthians about the Macedonian churches, Paul makes a direct link between their trials and their generous giving. He writes: 'Out of the most severe trial, their overflowing joy and their extreme poverty welled up in rich generosity' (2 Cor. 8:2). Let us ask the Lord to give us this same perspective as we walk through our trials. Even though they may cause us grief as we go through them, we can trust that they will have a positive and productive result in our lives, and for this reason we will rejoice.

Consider it pure joy … whenever you face trials
of many kinds, because you know that the testing of your
faith develops perseverance.
James 1:2–3

Trials

Many and varied are the trials
That we must face day after day
And how we shun them and abhor them,
These difficulties on life's way.

If all were calm and all contentment
What patient mortals we would be!
If life were but a bed of roses
None better would you see than me!

And yet, how fragile and how flimsy
Would be the worth of him who basks
In everlasting sunshine, without
Storms and tempests and hard tasks.

For, in his wisdom, God permits us
To bear affliction here and now,
In order to prepare for glory
Each one of us who to him bow.

Our faith will only know endurance,
Refined by fire, like all true gold.
And all-sufficient is his mercy
To keep his flock safe in the fold.

Lord, thank You that I can always count on Your presence even when I am
going through trials of various sorts. Thank You that difficulties that come
my way can produce positive qualities in my life. I pray for Christians who
are being persecuted for their faith. Keep them strong and faithful, Lord.

Personal Reflections

Walking by faith

We live by faith, not by sight.
2 Corinthians 5:7

As I was walking across a busy road in Geneva one day, a blind man with a white cane was crossing opposite me. As he reached the middle of the pedestrian crossing, he inadvertently swerved and started walking diagonally into the oncoming traffic. I gently touched his arm and explained where he was heading and proposed to guide him across the road. He had the faith to believe, even though he could not see where he was going, that I would get him safely onto the opposite pavement.

As we come to the end of our autumn readings and as we continue to walk with God each day, we are called upon to walk by faith. We cannot always see where we are going. We do not always understand what befalls us, but if we have entered into a relationship with God through Jesus, then we know that we can trust Him.

Can you say with Habakkuk, 'yet I will rejoice' (3:18), not just hang in there, but rejoice, even when there's nothing left? Similarly, can you say with Job, 'my eyes have seen you' (42:5), and be content with that?

What is your reaction in the face of bereavement, loss, illness, unemployment, or an uncertain future? Despair? Certainly, if all the hope we have is in this world alone and that hope crumbles, then – yes – despair would be the only alternative. '… Put your hope in God' (see Psa. 42:5,11) is the psalmist's answer to his downcast, disturbed soul.

The writer of the letter to the Hebrews gives a long list of those heroes of the faith who, thanks to God's intervention in their lives, accomplished mighty acts and performed wonders. There are too many to mention (see chapter 11:32–34). Great were their exploits, glorious their deeds!

What a shock, then, to read on: 'Others were tortured … Some faced jeers and flogging, while still others were chained and put in prison. They were stoned; they were sawn in two; they were put to death by the sword. They went about … destitute, persecuted and ill-treated' (Heb. 11:35b–37). Not much glory here! In many parts of today's world, things have not changed. Christians are still persecuted and put to death for their faith.

However, faith looks beyond the immediate, beyond the tragedies of this life to the 'something better' (see Heb. 11:40) that God has provided. Do you believe in this 'something better'? It is difficult for us to look past the here and now. The 'something better' in the future often escapes us.

If, as the writer to the Hebrews tells us, '… faith is being sure of what we hope for and certain of what we do not see' (11:1), then we can look by faith beyond our present circumstances to that 'eternal weight of glory' (NRSV) that our 'light and momentary troubles' are achieving for us (2 Cor. 4:17).

We can experience peace and joy and contentment here and now in the midst of suffering and pain, trials and tribulations, as we fix our eyes on Jesus. But we can also look beyond this world to a sure eternity where there will be 'no more death or mourning or crying or pain …' (Rev. 21:4).

> *… without faith it is impossible to please God …*
> Hebrews 11:6

Lord, I don't like problems and difficulties and pain! Yet, when I compare my situation to that of people in parts of the world where Christians are persecuted for their faith, or where they are caught up in conflict and war, or where they are subject to the result of natural disasters or terrorist attacks, or where there is no food, I realise that my trials are light in comparison. Whatever my situation, help me to look to You. My hope is in You, Lord. Strengthen me through the difficulties that come my way. Help me to walk by faith and see my present situation in the light of eternity.

Though the fig-tree does not bud
and there are no grapes on the vines,
though the olive crop fails
and the fields produce no food,
Though there are no sheep in the pen
and no cattle in the stalls,
yet I will rejoice in the LORD,
I will be joyful in God my Saviour.
Habakkuk 3:17–18

When I look beside me,
I see that there is no one to help me,
no one to protect me.
No one cares for me.
LORD, I cry to you for help;
you, LORD, are my protector;
you are all I want in this life.
Psalm 142:4–5, GNB

Faith

You, LORD, are all I have,
and you give me all I need
Psalm 16:5a, GNB

When friendship fails
And no one cares
That sorrow crushes me,
Think of the nails:
There's one who shares
The pain and agony.

Why look elsewhere
To find the love
That only he can give?
In deep despair,
Just glance above –
Look up at him and live.

A warm embrace,
A loving touch –
When these things are denied,

By God's own grace
I have so much
And in his peace abide.

Why comfort seek
From one who'll fall,
A loved one though he be?
When I am weak,
I can do all
Through Christ who strengthens me.

He's all I have,
This precious friend.
His is the voice I heed.
Whate'er I crave,
I can depend
On him to meet my need.

Personal Reflections

Winter

In the bleak mid-winter
Frosty wind made moan,
Earth stood hard as iron,
Water like a stone;
Snow had fallen, snow on snow,
Snow on snow,
In the bleak mid-winter
Long ago.[4]

The part of France where I live is near the Alps. People come from all over the country, as well as from other parts of Europe and elsewhere, to ski. The Mont Blanc is the highest mountain in the area. Culminating at 4,800 metres, its snowy summit stands out against the winter sky. The mountain can also be treacherous as, sadly, people lose their lives in avalanches.

This is the time of year that my husband puts out nuts and seeds for the birds. With his binoculars, he watches them balancing on the bare branches of the trees in our garden or hanging upside down on the nuts. He photographs them – sparrows, blue tits, coal tits, robins, blackbirds – against the backdrop of snow.

As we step into the cold of winter, with its shorter days and long, dark nights, we can count on God's presence as we continue to walk with Him. He will spread His warmth around us if we suffer the chill winter of the soul. He will guide us through the darkness and bring us out into His marvellous light. He will give us the faith to persevere and to endure through the storms of life and He will give us the assurance that He can meet all our needs.

Just as we can look beyond the winter to glimpse another spring on the horizon, so we can look beyond this life to a new dawn in eternity. The truths of God's Word are 'a light shining in a dark place, until the day dawns and the morning star rises in your hearts' (2 Pet. 1:19).

4. Christina Georgina Rossetti (1830–94).

Walking with God

*'So do not fear, for I am with you; do not be dismayed, for I am
your God. I will strengthen you and help you; I will uphold you
with my righteous right hand.'*
Isaiah 41:10

I t is a custom in some churches to print out a 'verse of the year' on a
card. This is given to members of the congregation at the beginning of
the year, and may be mailed to absent friends. Carmen, a member of
our church in Geneva, wrote to me soon after her arrival in Portugal where
she had gone to study the language before going out to Mozambique as a
missionary:

> When I arrived here, my first thought was, 'I don't know where my
> verse of the year is!' But I found it as I unpacked my bags. It is here
> beside me each day.

Several years ago, the above verse from the prophecy of Isaiah was the
verse of the year for our church. It was a daily reminder that we were
walking with God, and that we could count on His presence, strength, help
and upholding. We had no reason to fear. I remember being encouraged
at a women's meeting at that time, as several women testified to having
experienced the truth of this verse during difficult times. One shared how
she had known the Lord's joy in the pain of bereavement; another told us
how she had felt the Lord's presence in an ongoing illness; and another
said how she had known the Lord's peace when the future looked far from
bright. It moved me to see how these women were really experiencing the

truth of these words in their day-to-day living. They were indeed walking with God.

This verse does not just consist of beautiful words printed on a piece of paper. The words are real and they are true. Many of the verses in the Bible that tell us not to fear also include the statement that God is with us. In Genesis 26:24, God says to Isaac: 'Do not be afraid, for *I am with you.*' In Deuteronomy 20:1, we read: 'When you go to war against your enemies ... do not be afraid of them, because the LORD *your God ... will be with you.*' In Deuteronomy 31:6, Moses says to the people of Israel: '... Do not be afraid or terrified ... for *the* LORD *your God goes with you ...*' In 1 Chronicles 28:20, King David says to his son Solomon: '... Do not be afraid or discouraged, for *the* LORD *God, my God, is with you*' (my italics).

We read of two men in the Old Testament of whom it was specifically said that they 'walked with God'. Twice within three verses of Scripture we read that 'Enoch walked with God' (see Gen. 5:22,24). In the very next chapter we read that Noah 'walked with God' (Gen. 6:9). Can it also be said of you and me?

> *... what does the* LORD *require of you?*
> *To act justly and to love mercy*
> *and to walk humbly with your God.*
> Micah 6:8b

As I was examining my relationship with God one day, a flood of questions came into my mind:

- Why do I want to know God?
- Why do I want to love God?
- Why do I want to walk with God?
- Why do I want at all times to centre my thoughts on Him, to fix my eyes on Him?
- Why do I want to penetrate more deeply into an intimacy with Him?
- Why do I want to know His presence with me constantly?

Is it for His sake, or for mine?
Is it for His glory or for my happiness?
Are my longings for *Him*, or for what He might give me, for the Giver or for the gifts?

May God give me the grace, as I walk with Him, to focus on Him for His sake alone, and not for any 'benefits' that this may bring me.

He leads me in right paths *for his name's sake*.
Psalm 23:3, NRSV (my italics)

Personal Reflections

Walking in the dark

If I say, 'Surely the darkness will hide me and the night become light around me,' even the darkness will not be dark to you; the night will shine like the day, for darkness is as light to you.
Psalm 139:11–12

M y friend Annie shared how she was in her basement when the lights went out. Everything was pitch black. She couldn't see a thing. There was not even a glimmer of light. Such an experience can be quite frightening.

Do you sometimes feel you are walking in darkness like that? The circumstances of life have plunged you into a seemingly endless tunnel, where all is dim. You are depressed, confused, maybe in despair. You have embarked upon this week without hope. Life goes on and you see no way out of your situation.

It is to you that these words are addressed: 'Let him who walks in the dark, who has no light, trust in the name of the LORD and rely on his God' (Isa. 50:10b). Notice the first verb in this verse. The verb 'to walk' would indicate that life is not static. We are advancing, moving on.

At times we cannot see where we are going. All is dark. In order to emphasise the darkness, the prophet stresses that there is 'no light'. There is not a flicker, not a gleam, not a spark. Only complete blackness.

The prophet exhorts us to 'trust in the name of the LORD'. Even if the way seems dark to us, the Lord knows the way. Indeed, He *is* the way (John 14:6). So let us follow Him. He has lived this life on earth with all its suffering and anguish, and He is with us in our difficulties. 'Never will I leave you; never will I forsake you' is His promise to us (Heb. 13:5b).

The possessive adjective 'his' towards the end of Isaiah 50:10b ('... let him ... rely on *his* God') would indicate a personal relationship. Have you entered into a personal relationship with God through Jesus Christ? If so, you can step out into life and walk with Him, trusting in Him, relying on Him, following Him who is the way, the truth, and the life.

The world was in darkness at the time of Jesus' birth. True, the Stoics, the Epicureans and the mystery religions attempted in different ways to meet people's fundamental needs. All failed. A spirit of gloom and pessimism had settled over the human race. Isaiah had previously talked about 'distress and darkness and fearful gloom' and 'utter darkness' upon the earth (see Isa. 8:22).

It is into this darkness that the light shone. 'The people walking in darkness have seen a great light ...' prophesied Isaiah (9:2). 'The light shines in the darkness ...' exclaimed John (1:5). It is to this gloomy, pessimistic world that 'good news of great joy' is proclaimed – the announcement of the birth of a Saviour. And what the pagan gods, the Stoics, the Epicureans and the mystery religions were not able to do, Jesus Christ did! He saved the people from their sins and gave them hope and light and new life.

> [Jesus said,] 'I am the light of the world. Whoever follows me will never walk in darkness, but will have the light of life.'
> John 8:12b

Out of the darkness

Out of the darkness Jesus came
Out of the depths he spoke my name
He drew me with his loving hand
And on the rock he made me stand.

My fears were slain, my sight restored,
My joy regained; my heart adored
The One whose life for me was given,
Who opened up the gate of heaven.

Derek Adamsbaum

Thank You, Lord, that You are always there, even in my darkness. You continue to guide me. I thank You that I can rely on You, count on You, trust You, even when my sight is dim and all seems obscure. And I thank You too that You will lead me out of the darkness into Your wonderful light.

Personal Reflections

Walking in the light

For you have delivered me from death and my feet from stumbling,
that I may walk before God in the light of life.
Psalm 56:13

I n Australia's Red Centre, I had the privilege one winter's night of observing the stars with an astronomer. Because we were in the desert, far away from the lights of any town, the stars shone even more brightly in the dark sky.

We read in the prologue to John's Gospel, relative to Jesus' coming into the world that, 'The light shines in the darkness, and the darkness has never put it out' (John 1:5, GNB). We know that 'people love the darkness rather than the light, because their deeds are evil' (John 3:19, GNB), but God, in His mercy, has called us 'out of darkness into his wonderful light' (1 Pet. 2:9). 'Blessed are those who … walk in the light of your presence, O LORD' exclaims the psalmist (Psa. 89:15).

In order to see our way clearly, we need light. How wonderful to discover that God has provided us with that light – 'light will shine on your ways' (Job 22:28b). And the psalmist declares, 'Your word is a lamp to my feet and a light for my path' (Psa. 119:105). If the road is dark before us, let us open up the Word of God, which sheds light upon our pathway.

And Jesus says, 'I am the light of the world.' Twice He utters these same words in two consecutive chapters of the Bible. They are recorded for us in John's Gospel chapter 8, when He is teaching in the Temple, and then again in the following chapter, just before healing the man born blind (see John 9:5). 'I am the light of the world.' He reveals to people their spiritual condition and shows them the truth about themselves and about God. 'I am the light of the world. Whoever follows me will never walk in darkness, but will have the light of life' (John 8:12b).

Before leaving this world, Jesus said to His disciples, 'You are going to have the light just a little while longer. Walk while you have the light, before darkness overtakes you. The man who walks in the dark does not know where he is going. Put your trust in the light while you have it, so that you may become sons of light' (John 12:35–36a).

'For you were once darkness,' wrote Paul to the Ephesians, 'but now you are light in the Lord. Live as children of light' (Eph. 5:8). He explains that living in the light means living '… in all goodness, righteousness and truth' (Eph. 5:9).

As disciples of Christ, we are the light of the world (Matt. 5:14). We are to live in communion with God. We are to live according to the truth. Have you ever noticed the strong link between living in the light and loving one's fellow believer? 'Anyone who claims to be in the light but hates his brother is still in the darkness. Whoever loves his brother lives in the light' (1 John 2:9–10a). May we be lights in this dark world as we trust God and walk in His ways, and as we reflect Jesus Christ and show love to our brothers and sisters.

… let us walk in the light of the LORD.
Isaiah 2:5

O Light, that followest all my way,
I yield my flickering torch to Thee;
My heart restores its borrowed ray,
That in Thy sunshine's blaze its day
May brighter, fairer be.

George Matheson
1842–1906

How good it is to know, Lord, that You are my light and my salvation! Thank You for Your Word, which is a lamp to my feet and a light to my path. Thank You for calling me out of darkness into Your wonderful light. Help me at all times to walk in the light of Your presence.

In the description of the New Jerusalem, we read that:

The city does not need the sun or the moon to shine on it, for the glory of God gives it light, and the Lamb is its lamp. The nations will walk by its light …

Revelation 21:23–24a

Personal Reflections

Walking with endurance

Let us fix our eyes on Jesus, the author and perfecter of our faith,
who for the joy set before him endured the cross, scorning its shame,
and sat down at the right hand of the throne of God.
Hebrews 12:2

One day, as I was walking to the shops, a little boy with a balloon came running along the pavement towards me, an expression of pure bliss and happiness on his face. As he passed me, he gave me a beautiful smile. My heart contracted as I thought of the pain and sorrow that life will inevitably bring to that carefree little soul (beginning probably with a burst balloon!). He will certainly be called upon to endure temptations and testings in his life.

Paul wrote to Timothy: 'Endure hardship with us like a good soldier of Christ Jesus' (2 Tim. 2:3). As I watched the child playing with his balloon, once again I thought how impossible life would be without God, and how much we need Him all the time.

When we think of all the 'burst balloons' in our lives – disappointments, failure, sin, loss – with all the accompanying pain, heartache, distress and grief, how thankful we can be for such a loving heavenly Father, who comforts, redeems, forgives, encourages, strengthens and, above all, gives us the option of looking at all of life's trials in the light of eternity, where there will be '… no more death or mourning or crying or pain …' (Rev. 21:4).

In the meantime, we are called to persevere. We are encouraged to endure the difficulties that come our way, as Abraham did. For we read in Hebrews 6:15 that '… Abraham, having patiently endured, obtained the promise' (NRSV).

A young Christian called Jeyaraj was arrested by the police in Sri Lanka and was imprisoned for nearly fourteen months for a crime he had not committed. He experienced the presence and love of God even in the midst of much pain and torture – an example of persecutions endured by believers in Jesus Christ in the twenty-first century.

Peter wrote: 'But if you suffer for doing good and you endure it, this is commendable before God' (1 Pet. 2:20). Paul makes clear to Timothy that in order to receive the wreath or the crown, the athlete must compete 'according to the rules' (2 Tim. 2:5b). In order to receive our reward in heaven, the Christian who is saved by grace must live this life in a way that is consistent with the teaching of God's Word. For this, we need to walk with endurance.

We are to keep our eyes on Jesus '… who endured … opposition from sinful men …' and we too are to 'Endure hardship as discipline' (Heb. 12:3,7a). The passage tells us clearly that 'No discipline seems pleasant at the time, but painful. Later on, however, it produces a harvest of righteousness and peace for those who have been trained by it' (Heb. 12:11). We are exhorted to make level paths for our feet (Heb. 12:13) as we walk with endurance.

But he who endures to the end will be saved.
Matthew 10:22, RSV

Jesus endured to the end, so that He was able to say 'It is finished' (see John 19:30):

It is finished

'It is finished.' A grateful sigh?
Mockery, insults, pain and buffeting.
Betrayal, hitting, denial, flogging.
Finished? Ended? All over with?

What is finished? He came to die.

Completed – the task he was given.
Accomplished – the ministry for which he was destined.
Fulfilled – the purpose for which he became man.

'It is finished!' A triumphant cry!

It is true, Lord, that we find it difficult to persevere and to endure. We can so easily give up. Thank You for the encouragement you give us in Your Word. Thank You that You can keep us from falling. Thank You too that You endured, and that You finished the work You came to do.

Personal Reflections

Walking alone

The Lord God said, 'It is not good for the man to be alone.
I will make a helper suitable for him.'
Genesis 2:18

Particularly in our western culture, we tend to be very individualistic. Many people choose to live alone. Others have no choice in the matter and are just plain lonely. However, that is not how God intended it to be. Having created man in His own image, God said it was not 'good' that he should be alone, so He created another human being – woman – to come to his rescue, and be one with him.

We all need to feel we belong … to someone, to some place, to something. To belong means to be a part of, to be attached to, to be connected with. Not to belong means to be alone, to be isolated, to be lonely. And loneliness is a problem faced by many people throughout the world. Scratch beneath the surface of any city and you will find lonely people hurting because they are alone and do not belong. They may not belong for a variety of reasons. They may not be the 'right' nationality, or the 'right' colour or race, or in the 'right' salary bracket or 'class'. They are alone, without friends, and some of them are without God. Lost.

And yet there is hope for such as these. Did not Jesus say He had come to 'seek and to save' the lost (Luke 19:10)? He told His disciples the following parables. In both cases, there was much rejoicing when that which was lost was found again:

> 'Suppose one of you has a hundred sheep and loses one of them.
> Does he not leave the ninety-nine in the open country and go after

the lost sheep until he finds it? And when he finds it, he joyfully puts it on his shoulders and goes home. Then he calls his friends and neighbours together and says, "Rejoice with me; I have found my lost sheep."'

Luke 15:3–6

'Or suppose a woman has ten silver coins and loses one. Does she not light a lamp, sweep the house and search carefully until she finds it? And when she finds it, she calls her friends and neighbours together and says, "Rejoice with me; I have found my lost coin."'

Luke 15:8–9

Just as Jesus reached out with compassion to lost souls around Him, so we as members of His Body, are to reach out and draw these lonely ones to Him, so that they too might belong and no longer walk alone.

You will leave me all alone.
Yet I am not alone, for my Father is with me.
John 16:32b

What a privilege it is, Lord, to spend time alone with You. With You, I am never really alone, because You have promised always to be with me. I pray for the lonely people in the world. May they be drawn to You and into fellowship with Your Church.

'… There was once a man who had two sons. The younger said to his father, "Father, I want right now what's coming to me."

So the father divided the property between them. It wasn't long before the younger son packed his bags and left for a distant

country. There, undisciplined and dissipated, he wasted everything
he had. After he had gone through all his money, there was a bad
famine all through that country and he began to hurt. He signed on
with a citizen there who assigned him to his fields to slop the pigs.
He was so hungry he would have eaten the corncobs in the pig slop,
but no one would give him any.

'That brought him to his senses. He said, "All those farmhands
working for my father sit down to three meals a day, and here I
am starving to death. I'm going back to my father. I'll say to him,
'Father, I've sinned against God, I've sinned before you; I don't
deserve to be called your son. Take me on as a hired hand.'" He got
right up and went home to his father.

'When he was still a long way off, his father saw him. His heart
pounding, he ran out, embraced him, and kissed him. The son
started his speech: "Father, I've sinned against God, I've sinned
before you; I don't deserve to be called your son ever again."

'But the father wasn't listening. He was calling to the servants,
"Quick. Bring a clean set of clothes and dress him. Put the family
ring on his finger and sandals on his feet. Then get a grain-fed heifer
and roast it. We're going to feast! We're going to have a wonderful
time! My son is here – given up for dead and now alive! Given up for
lost and now found!" And they began to have a wonderful time.'

Luke 15:11–24, The Message

Alone – with God

When mountain peaks in splendour rise
Above the misty valley
And snow in drifts before me lies
I long to dilly-dally

To spend an hour or two alone
Just lost in contemplation
Before this scene that is my own
In its vast desolation

Where all around the softness dulls
The senses and each motion
While in the air the screaming gulls
Exult in wild devotion

For surely God is in this place
Of solitude and bleakness.
I lift my heart to seek his face
And bow my head in meekness.

Personal Reflections

Walking together

Do two walk together unless they have agreed to do so?
Amos 3:3

Samuel, a former elder of the church we worked with in Geneva, went back provisionally to his home country of Tanzania to make contact with a group of 500 Tanzanian Christians who had come together in the village where Samuel's family originated, with the desire of starting a church. Samuel went to minister to this community of believers.

'Togetherness' has been a characteristic of Christians right from the beginning. In the book of Acts we read, 'When the day of Pentecost came, they were all *together* in one place. … All the believers were *together* and had everything in common. … Every day they continued to meet *together* in the temple courts. They broke bread in their homes and ate *together* with glad and sincere hearts' (Acts 2:1,44,46, my italics).

Paul reminds us that '… we who are many form one body, and each member belongs to all the others' (Rom. 12:5). 'If one part suffers, every part suffers with it; if one part is honoured, every part rejoices with it' (1 Cor. 12:26). This is true community – working together, serving together, suffering together, rejoicing together.

Praying together is a great privilege and one which has a special promise. For Jesus said: '… if two of you on earth agree about anything you ask for, it will be done for you by my Father in heaven. For where two or three come together in my name, there am I with them' (Matt. 18:19–20).

We have a wonderful example, in the book of Acts chapter 12, of Christians met together to pray for Peter who was in prison. The prayers were effective and God answered. 'The Lord sent his angel to rescue me' acknowledged Peter, when he eventually 'realized what had happened to him' (Acts 12:11, GNB). Immediately he went to the house of Mary, the mother of John Mark 'where many people had gathered and were praying' (Acts 12:12, GNB) – 'they were amazed' (Acts 12:16, GNB) and could not believe that it was really Peter who was knocking at the door! Peter 'explained to them how the Lord had brought him out of prison' (Acts 12:17, GNB). What a tremendous answer to their prayers!

It is amazing how often the phrases 'one another' and 'each other' appear in the Scripture passages relative to the Church, the Body of Christ. 'Love one another' (1 Pet. 1:22), 'Live in harmony with one another' (Rom. 12:16), 'Offer hospitality to one another' (1 Pet. 4:9), 'wash one another's feet' (John 13:14), 'carry each other's burdens' (Gal. 6:2), 'pray for each other' (James 5:16), 'encourage one another and build each other up' (1 Thess. 5:11), 'Live in peace with each other' (1 Thess. 5:13), 'be kind to each other' (1 Thess. 5:15), 'serve one another' (Gal. 5:13).

God did not intend for us to live in isolation. We are meant to be in relationship with one another, walking in fellowship with other believers. Walking together.

> *Therefore encourage one another and build each other up, just as*
> *in fact you are doing. ... Live in peace with each other. And we urge*
> *you, brothers, warn those who are idle, encourage the timid,*
> *help the weak, be patient with everyone. ... always try to be kind*
> *to each other and to everyone else.*
> 1 Thessalonians 5:11,13–15

Thank You, Lord for my church. Thank You for being able to enjoy fellowship with other believers. Thank You that we are able to meet together and worship You together, that we can pray together and study Your Word together. May we be a blessing and an encouragement to one another.

Together

Warmth and companionship
Silent togetherness
Hearts and fingers entwined
Complete understanding
Both of same purpose
One in heart and in mind.

Outside – desolation
Bleakness, destruction
Dull and windy and cold –
Inspires intercession
United and heartfelt
Vital, tender and bold.

Comforting friendship
Thoughts intermingled
Oh! that time would stand still!
Expressed in a handclasp
Love and communion
Joy that time cannot kill.

Personal Reflections

Walking confidently and courageously

Let us ... approach the throne of grace with boldness ...
Hebrews 4:16, NRSV

How do you feel at the beginning of this week? Positive? On top of things? Or unhappy because of your circumstances? Fearful of the future? Take heart! You have a heavenly Father, who wants the best for you. Nothing is beyond His control.

'Are not two sparrows sold for a penny?' asked Jesus. 'Yet not one of them will fall to the ground apart from the will of your Father. ... So don't be afraid; you are worth more than many sparrows' (Matt. 10:29,31).

Sparrows are 'two a penny' – in many places anyway and certainly round our way. (Apparently they are now in danger of extinction in London, which is a shame.) I can look out of my window any day and I will see sparrows in great number. In winter, we have seeds and nuts hanging from some of the trees in our garden, and although not quite such clever acrobats as the tits, the sparrows make sure they get their share!

God has His eye on them, numerous as they are. If nothing can happen to a sparrow without His knowing it, then you can be sure He is watching over you who are worth a lot more than those little birds. He tells you not to be afraid. God is in control both of your present circumstances and as far as the future is concerned.

If your hope is in God, you can walk by faith and rise above the circumstances, no matter how painful or how bleak. Already in this world, we can experience His love, His strength, and His compassion. He can meet our deepest needs here and now: '... in all these things we are more than conquerors through him who loved us' (Rom. 8:37). Paul claimed that he had '... learned the secret of being content in any and every situation ...' (Phil. 4:12).

As we learn to depend on God, He gives us the boldness and confidence to confront the situations that we face in life. There are several instances recorded for us in Scripture where the early disciples were given the courage to speak out for their Lord. When Peter and John appeared before the Sanhedrin after healing a crippled beggar, we read that the religious leaders were astonished 'When they saw the courage of Peter and John' (Acts 4:13a).

We read too that when Paul was in Jerusalem, he moved around 'preaching boldly in the name of the Lord' (Acts 9:28b, GNB). In a later chapter of the book of Acts, we see Apollos begin '... to speak boldly in the synagogue' (Acts 18:26, GNB). And when he was in Ephesus, 'Paul went into the synagogue and during three months spoke boldly with the people' (Acts 19:8a, GNB). Later, in a letter to the Christians in Ephesus, Paul asked them to pray that when he spoke, he would '... fearlessly make known the mystery of the gospel ... Pray that I may declare it fearlessly ...' (Eph. 6:19b–20).

But what is even more amazing is that we who are sinners can come with boldness into God's presence because He sees us as clothed in the righteousness of Christ: '... we have confidence to enter the Most Holy Place by the blood of Jesus' (Heb. 10:19).

> ... God has said, 'Never will I leave you; never will I forsake you.'
> So we say with confidence, 'The Lord is my helper; I will not be
> afraid. What can man do to me?'
> Hebrews 13:5–6

How wonderful it is, Lord, to be able to count on You. Thank You that You will never leave me or forsake me. In you I can be bold and strong and courageous to accomplish Your purposes here on earth. Thank You for watching over me and protecting me.

God spoke to Joshua as He was about to lead the Israelites into the promised land. He said:

> As I was with Moses, so I will be with you; I will not fail you or forsake you. Be strong and courageous; for you shall put this people in possession of the land that I swore to their ancestors to give them. Only be strong and very courageous … This book of the law shall not depart from out of your mouth; you shall meditate on it day and night, so that you may be careful to act in accordance with all that is written in it. For then you shall make your way prosperous, and then you shall be successful. I hereby command you: Be strong and courageous; do not be frightened or dismayed, for the Lord your God is with you wherever you go.
>
> Joshua 1:5–9, NRSV

Personal Reflections

Walking from death to life

When you were dead in your sins …
God made you alive with Christ …
Colossians 2:13

The Scriptures are very clear in describing our spiritual state. There is no beating about the bush, no possible misunderstanding, no false hope given. We are either *dead* or *alive* (Col. 2:13). In our natural state, we are spiritually dead. We are alienated from God because of our sin (Col. 1:21).

God made Jesus Christ, the spotless Lamb of God '… who had no sin to be sin for us' (2 Cor. 5:21a). He took our sins upon Himself and bore the penalty – death on the cross – in our place, so that we might pass from death to life, clothed in His righteousness, and be reconciled to God.

But this transformation is not automatic. The choice is ours. We can choose to remain 'dead', 'slaves to sin' (Rom. 6:17) and alienated from God. How tragic that some choose to remain in their sin, for this means that their separation from God will be for eternity.

Choosing Christ, on the other hand, leads to eternal life. Jesus wisely exhorts us, however, to 'estimate the cost' (Luke 14:28) before making our choice. The Christian life is one where we turn our back on sin. It is a life of total commitment to Jesus Christ, a life of obedience to Him. 'Jesus said … "If anyone would come after me, he must deny himself and take up his cross daily and follow me"' (Luke 9:23).

For some, this decision to follow Jesus involves a real struggle, for the pleasures of sin seem very attractive and the pull of the world is strong. But, whereas the pleasures of sin are fleeting and lead to death, the blessings of obedience are eternal.

The road may not always be easy though, as the following words of Jesus would indicate: 'Enter through the narrow gate. For wide is the gate and broad is the road that leads to destruction, and many enter through it. But small is the gate and narrow the road that leads to life, and only a few find it' (Matt. 7:13–14).

Maybe we are hesitant about taking this step because we are afraid that we will not be able to follow through on our commitment. It is true that we cannot live the Christian life in our own strength. But when we accept Jesus Christ, we become indwelt by the Holy Spirit who gives us the power to lead a life pleasing to God.

The choice is ours. Remember Joshua's challenge to the people of Israel: '… choose for yourselves this day whom you will serve … But as for me and my household, we will serve the LORD' (Josh. 24:15). The alternative to serving the Lord would have been to serve 'the gods of the Amorites'. Are we going to serve the gods of this world or will we serve the Lord?

> *… I have set before you life and death …*
> *Now choose life, so that you … may live …*
> Deuteronomy 30:19

Lord God, thank You for dying for me. Thank You too that I can share in Your resurrection life and victory. I have new life in You. I have passed from death to life. I praise You, Lord.

Once when large crowds of people were going along with Jesus, he turned and said to them, 'Whoever comes to me cannot be my disciple unless he loves me more than he loves his father and his mother, his wife and his children, his brothers and his sisters, and himself as well. Whoever does not carry his own cross and come after me cannot be my disciple.

'If one of you is planning to build a tower, he sits down first and works out what it will cost, to see if he has enough money to finish the job. If he doesn't, he will not be able to finish the tower after laying the foundation; and all who see what happened will laugh at him. "This man began to build but can't finish the job!" they will say.

'If a king goes out with ten thousand men to fight another king who comes against him with twenty thousand men, he will sit down first and decide if he is strong enough to face that other king. If he isn't, he will send messengers to meet the other king, to ask for terms of peace while he is still a long way off. In the same way,' concluded Jesus, 'none of you can be my disciple unless he gives up everything he has.'

Luke 14:25–33, GNB

Long my imprisoned spirit lay
Fast bound in sin and nature's night;
Thine eye diffused a quickening ray,
I woke, the dungeon flamed with light;
My chains fell off, my heart was free;
I rose, went forth, and followed Thee.

No condemnation now I dread;
Jesus, and all in Him, is mine!
Alive in Him, my living Head,
And clothed in righteousness divine,
Bold I approach the eternal throne,
And claim the crown, through Christ my own.

Charles Wesley
1707–88

Come, heavy souls, oppressed that are
With doubts, and fears, and carking care.
Lay all your burdens down, and see
There's one that carried once a tree
Upon his back, and, which is more,
A heavier weight, your sins, he bore.
Think then how easily he can
Your sorrows bear that's God and man;
Think too how willing he's to take
Your care on him, who for your sake
Sweat bloody drops, prayed, fasted, cried,
Was bound, scoured, mocked, crucified.
He that so much for you did do,
Will do yet more, and care for you.

Thomas Washbourne
1606–87

Personal Reflections

Walking through storms

You have been a refuge for the poor, a refuge for the needy
in his distress, a shelter from the storm …
Isaiah 25:4

This childhood rhyme came into my mind on a cold, windy winter's day:

> The March wind doth blow
> And we shall have snow.
> And what will poor robin do then, poor thing?
> He'll sit in a barn
> And keep himself warm
> And hide his head under his wing, poor thing.

Wind, snow, rain or hail, robins round our way – together with sparrows, tits, chaffinches, blackbirds, and even a pair of turtle doves – seem ready enough to hold their heads high and brave the elements! No hiding in barns for them! Maybe their intrepid confrontation with nature has something to do with the nuts and seeds hanging from our sycamore tree! Be that as it may, there they are, not running away from, but courageously facing the winds and storms.

I wonder how you measure up to those little birds. At the first sign of hardship, do you run away and hide with your head under your metaphorical wing? Or do you courageously face the storms of life, with head held high?

Maybe the storm is within and is caused by your 'sinful nature with its passions and desires' (Gal. 5:24b), making you hang your head in shame. Perhaps it is without and takes the form of trials and sorrows that come upon you unbidden causing you to suffer in solitude and silence.

But our hope and trust must always be in Jesus. We must never lose sight of eternal realities, so that when tragedy does strike, when sorrow does come upon us, our faith will not waver and our foundation will stand firm.

No matter what the origin of the storm may be, if you are in Christ, having come to know Him as your Saviour and acknowledge Him as your Lord, you can know His peace. You can stand tall and face it head on assured of forgiveness and cleansing and victory over sin, confident of His presence with you, knowing that His 'power is made perfect in weakness' (2 Cor. 12:9).

The striking description of a storm, given to us by Luke who accompanied Paul on his journey to Rome, enables us almost to feel the violence of the wind and the pounding of the waves: '… a wind of hurricane force … swept down from the island. The ship was caught by the storm and could not head into the wind; so we gave way to it and were driven along' (Acts 27:14–15). The tempest raged to such a degree, and the ship was so violently battered that first the cargo and afterwards 'the ship's tackle' (v.19) were thrown overboard. And then, says Luke, 'When neither sun nor stars appeared for many days and the storm continued raging, we finally gave up all hope of being saved' (v.20).

Have you ever felt like giving up all hope in the storms of life? There seems to be no solution to the problems you are facing. You can feel yourself sinking deeper and deeper into discouragement and despair and depression.

Let us see how Paul's sea voyage finished up. First of all, he urged the men to keep up their courage. Even though the ship would be wrecked, Paul assured them that no lives would be lost. How could he be so sure? God had revealed it to him by an angel (see v.23). This was a good opportunity for Paul to witness to his faith, as he made a point of saying that this was the God to whom he belonged and whom he served and worshipped. God's purposes for Paul would be accomplished. And the message continued: '… God has graciously given you the lives of all who sail with you' (v.24).

And Paul added '… I have faith in God …' (v.25).

Do you have faith in God? Trust Him then to enable you to walk through the storms of life. His purposes for you will be fulfilled, so 'keep up your courage' (Acts 27:25).

One day Jesus got into a boat with his disciples and said to them,
'Let us go across to the other side of the lake.' So they started out.
As they were sailing, Jesus fell asleep. Suddenly a strong wind blew
down on the lake, and the boat began to fill with water, so that they
were all in great danger. The disciples went to Jesus and woke him
up, saying, 'Master, Master! We are about to die!'
Jesus got up and gave an order to the wind and the stormy water;
they died down, and there was a great calm.
Luke 8:22–24, GNB

Thank You, Lord, that I can count on Your presence through all the storms of life. I know I can count on Your protection. You command the wind and the waves and they obey You. You will keep me safe and bring me into Your heavenly harbour.

The storm

Lightning flashing
Thunder crashing
Wind slashing
Branches thrashing
Trees smashing
Hillside gashing
Rain lashing
Puddles splashing
People dashing
Teeth gnashing

Psalm 107

Some went down to the sea in ships,
doing business on the mighty waters;
they saw the deeds of the LORD*,*
his wondrous works in the deep.
For he commanded and raised the stormy wind,
which lifted up the waves of the sea.
They mounted up to heaven, they went down to the depths;
their courage melted away in their calamity;
they reeled and staggered like drunkards,
and were at their wits' end.
Then they cried to the LORD *in their trouble,*
and he brought them out from their distress;
he made the storm be still,
and the waves of the sea were hushed.
Then they were glad because they had quiet,
and he brought them to their desired haven.
verses 23–30, NRSV

Personal Reflections

Walking with perseverance

*Therefore, since we are surrounded by such a great cloud of
witnesses, let us throw off everything that hinders and the sin that so
easily entangles, and let us run with perseverance the race marked
out for us. Let us fix our eyes on Jesus …*
Hebrews 12:1–2a

'Don't try to convert me!' was Evelyne's parting shot. A confessed
atheist, this French schoolteacher resisted my attempts to share
the gospel with her. Now – thirty years later – retired, no longer
an atheist, but not yet a Christian, she is more willing to listen. I could
however, have given up long ago. Paul tells Timothy to 'proclaim the
message; be persistent, whether the time is favourable or unfavourable'
(2 Tim. 4:2a, NRSV).

I still remember, as a child at school, excitedly embarking upon a new
activity: weaving. I confess to my shame that the initial enthusiasm soon
wore off and I never did finish the piece of work I had so readily begun. I
lacked perseverance.

It is sometimes difficult, after having begun the Christian life with much
enthusiasm, to maintain the momentum. Many times in Scripture we are
urged to continue, to keep going, to persevere in one or other aspect of
Christian living.

The above quotation from the letter to the Hebrews exhorts us to take
courage from those believers who have gone before. With this mighty 'cloud
of witnesses' cheering us on, we are to run the race with perseverance and
with no distractions, keeping our eyes on the finishing line … where Jesus,
the One who ran the race before us, is waiting.

I play tennis. I know that if I want to win, I need to keep my eye on the ball and concentrate fully on the game. No distracting thoughts are permitted. No gazing at the scenery. The French Open Tennis Tournament in Paris in 2004 chalked up a record for persevering play. As there is no tie-break in the fifth set, one match went on for over six hours!

What kind of distractions could cause us to falter in the race? The above verse mentions two: 'everything that hinders' and 'the sin that so easily entangles'. 'Everything that hinders' could be anything that holds us back in the Christian life, preventing us from spiritual growth or from experiencing all that God longs to give us. The second distraction, 'sin', while more easily definable, is perhaps more difficult to throw off. It 'clings so closely' (NRSV). We need to take radical steps to turn away from our sin and to turn to God in repentance and faith. Difficult though the race may be, Jesus has run it before us. He will be with us to strengthen us and to enable us not only to *walk*, but to '*run* with perseverance' (my italics)!

> *Pray at all times in the Spirit, with all prayer and supplication.*
> *To that end keep alert with all perseverance,*
> *making supplication for all the saints …*
> Ephesians 6:18, RSV

Jesus told His disciples a story to teach them that they should persevere in prayer:

> 'There was once a judge in some city who never gave God a thought and cared nothing for people. A widow in that city kept after him: "My rights are being violated. Protect me!"
>
> 'He never gave her the time of day. But after this went on and on he said to himself, "I care nothing what God thinks, even less what people think. But because this widow won't quit badgering me, I'd better do something and see that she gets justice – otherwise I'm going to end up beaten black-and-blue by her pounding."'

Jesus concluded His story by asking His disciples,

> 'But how much of that kind of persistent faith will the Son of Man find on the earth when he returns?'
>
> Luke 18:2–8, The Message

He who would valiant be
'Gainst all disaster,
Let him in constancy
Follow the Master.
There's no discouragement
Shall make him once relent
His first avowed intent
To be a pilgrim.

John Bunyan
1628–88

Forgive me, Lord, for giving up and for being distracted so easily. Increase my faith and enable me to persevere both in running the race and also in prayer. Help me to keep my eyes fixed on You.

Personal Reflections

Walking through suffering

Rejoice that you participate in the sufferings of Christ …
1 Peter 4:13

'Isn't God supposed to make me happy?' asked Theresa, voicing a question which is perhaps at the back of many people's minds. But nowhere do the Scriptures imply that life is a bed of roses. Sure, the Bible talks of joy, peace, hope and eternal life. All these are ours in Christ. But the Bible never hides the fact that we may suffer.

There is one thing we will never escape from in this life, and that is suffering – in one form or another. Neither physical suffering, nor moral suffering can be avoided. Most people are bereaved at least once – and usually several times – in their lifetime. We all fall ill at one time or another.

We only need to listen to the News to realise that each day many people undergo severe pain. Wars, terrorist attacks, natural disasters, accidents, all cause untold suffering. A letter that we received in May 2004 from some missionary friends reflected that 'Remembering the sufferings of Christ in the first-century world gives us strength and courage to face the world that we live in today'.

Even though Jesus promised us a life of fulfilment, He never indicated that it would be easy or free from suffering. On the contrary, He said, 'If anyone would come after me, he must deny himself and take up his cross daily and follow me' (Luke 9:23b).

On another occasion, He spelled out more fully what is involved in being a disciple. 'If anyone comes to me and does not hate his father and mother, his wife and children, his brothers and sisters – yes, even his own life – he cannot be my disciple. And anyone who does not carry his cross and follow me cannot be my disciple' (Luke 14:26–27). He encourages us to count the cost before committing ourselves. And there is a cost. Jesus calls us to a life of sacrifice and renunciation and self-denial.

Some years ago, Jim, a member of our church, gave up a good position in a multinational company in Geneva, because he was expected to act in a way that was not possible for him as a Christian. With a wife and four children to support, Jim's decision was not made lightly. But he made the sacrifice because he wanted to follow Jesus wholeheartedly.

In the early chapters of the book of Acts, we see the apostles, full of the Holy Spirit, proclaiming the good news of salvation in Jesus. The authorities and religious leaders persecute them, flog them, imprison them and threaten them. But they persist in preaching the gospel. 'We must obey God rather than men!' they exclaim (Acts 5:29b). They left the Sanhedrin, 'rejoicing because they had been counted worthy of suffering disgrace for the Name' (Acts 5:41b).

But some of our suffering is of our own making. 'Oh! what needless pain we bear' says the old hymn.[5] I have prayed so often and so long for deliverance from sin. And yet when I look into my heart, I see that self is at the root of my sinful nature. God has not promised deliverance from self. I have to die to self.

Peter tells us not to '… be surprised at the painful trial you are suffering … But rejoice that you participate in the sufferings of Christ' (1 Pet. 4:12–13). He says that trials that come our way can strengthen and purify our faith, and that 'These have come so that your faith – of greater worth than gold, which perishes even though refined by fire – may be proved genuine and may result in praise, glory and honour when Jesus Christ is revealed' (1 Pet. 1:7). He encourages us to look beyond the sufferings of this life to the '… new birth into a living hope … and into an inheritance … kept in heaven for [us]' (1 Pet. 1:3–4).

---

5. Joseph Scriven (1819–86), *What a friend we have in Jesus.*

*It is commendable if a man bears up under the pain of unjust
suffering because he is conscious of God. … But if you suffer for
doing good and you endure it, this is commendable before God.*

1 Peter 2:19–20

Lord, teach me what it means to take up my cross daily. Show me what You
want me to learn through the suffering in my life.

Suffering

When you're feeling down
And not very bright
And you're in the dark
And your heart's not right

When you feel alone
In the dead of night,
To whom can you turn
To explain your plight?

There is One who cares
And he's filled with might.
He'll draw close to you
So you'll win the fight.

He'll not let you go
But he'll hold you tight
And he'll bring you through
To wonderful light.

Personal Reflections

Walking regretfully

… God … commands all people everywhere to repent.
Acts 17:30

I n Geneva, Switzerland, just across the border from where I live in France, there are many expatriates. People are transferred there primarily for professional reasons. Many work in large multinational companies, or at the UN or in other international organisations. This kind of relocation is often a time of uprooting and difficult upheaval. It involves adapting to a new country, a new language, and a new school system for the children. Many of these people are homesick and look back longingly to the 'good old days'. They find it hard to settle and adjust. 'If only we could have stayed at home!' they murmur. 'If only things weren't so complicated!'

'If only …' How many times have we pronounced these words? They express regret, the wish that things were or had been different. They also wistfully imply the inevitability of what now is. It is no good saying 'If only …' We must accept that things are as they are and take it from there. We must bring God into the situation as it now stands. We can pour out to Him all our pain and heartache and longing, all our regrets and desires. He is in control of all things. He can transform situations. More importantly perhaps, He can change *us* as we learn to come to terms with our situation. Can we not trust that His way is best?

But what if the circumstances are a result of our own sin, folly or error? 'If only I had not done that!' 'If only I had not said such an unkind thing!' 'If only I had behaved differently!' Even then God can redeem the situation and bring good out of evil. Not with a magical wave of a wand, however. If we need to repent, we know that we can count on His forgiveness.

When the apostles began preaching the gospel after Jesus was taken up to heaven and after He had sent His Spirit at Pentecost, their message was simply, 'Repent and be baptised' (Acts 2:38). 'Repent … and turn to God, so that your sins may be wiped out' (Acts 3:19).

But that does not necessarily mean that we will not have to face the consequences of our unkind words or sinful actions. The way may be regretfully long and painful. But it can be a learning process that will bring forth much fruit. God does not usually deal in instant remedies. But He will meet us in our suffering and pain and bring us through to a joyful experience of Himself and a life of fulfilment here on earth, and the glorious assurance of heaven.

> *… repentance and forgiveness of sins will be preached*
> *in [Christ's] name to all nations …*
> Luke 24:47

Forgive me, Lord. I come to You now in repentance and faith. I deeply regret my sin. Cleanse me, Lord. I ask You to come into my life and transform me.

If only

If I might only love my God and die!
But now He bids me love Him and live on,
Now when the bloom of all my life is gone,
The pleasant half of life has quite gone by.
The tree of hope is lopped that spread so high;
And I forget how summer glowed and shone,
When autumn grips me with its fingers wan,
And frets me with its fitful windy sigh.
When autumn passes then must winter numb,
And winter may not pass a weary while,
But when it passes spring shall flower again:
And in that spring who weepeth now shall smile,
Yea, they shall wax who now are on the wane,
Yea, they shall sing for love when Christ shall come.

Christina Georgina Rossetti
1830–94

Personal Reflections

WEEK 52

Walking with assurance

*… let us draw near to God with a sincere heart
in full assurance of faith …*
Hebrews 10:22a

What a difference it makes to know the Lord! Knowing Him, walking with Him, really does transform our attitude and change our life. As we mentioned in the Preface, the themes of the meditations in this book overlap. That is because God meets all our needs. Our life is a whole and we depend on Him. It is not surprising, then, that when we ask for strength, He also gives us hope, and that the hope He gives us is in fact the blessed assurance we referred to earlier in this book. When we request His forgiveness, He also gives us his joy; when we pray for comfort, He gives us peace as well; when we need to persevere, He gives us the strength to endure.

As a conclusion to our walking together each day in paths of peace and in the pleasant ways of wisdom, I have attempted to enumerate some of God's blessings to us. I have tried to show how He meets our needs:

When we are weak,
He gives us His strength.

When we are confused,
He gives us His wisdom.

When we are perplexed,
He gives us His understanding.

When we are depressed,
He gives us hope.

When we are lonely,
He assures us of His presence.

When we are sad or grieving,
He consoles and comforts us.

When we sorrow,
He gives us His joy.

When we are unsure,
He guides and directs us.

When we are vulnerable,
He protects us.

When we sin,
He forgives and cleanses us.

When we are rejected,
He loves us with unfailing love.

When we are troubled,
He gives us His peace.

When we draw near to Him,
He draws near to us.

The above thoughts are based on the following Bible verses:
2 Corinthians 12:9–10; Philippians 4:13; James 1:5; Proverbs 4:11; Proverbs
3:5–6; Psalm 42:5,11; 43:5; Hebrews 13:5; Psalm 23:4; Isaiah 66:13; Psalm
126:5–6; Psalm 30:5; Isaiah 30:21; Psalm 23:3; Psalm 17:8; Psalm 18:2;
1 John 1:9; Romans 8:35; 1 John 3:1; John 14:1,27; Philippians 4:6–7;
James 4:8

Blessed assurance

Blesséd assurance – Jesus is mine!
O what a foretaste of glory divine!
Heir of salvation, purchase of God;
Born of his Spirit, washed in his blood.

Fanny J. Crosby
1820–1915

Thank You, Lord, for meeting all of my needs. Thank You that I can walk closely with You each day, in fullness of joy. Thank You for enabling me to walk in love and in a spirit of forgiveness. Thank You for Your mercy and grace and strength and wisdom. Thank You, too, for the hard times You permit me to go through, because through them You teach me to persevere and to endure and to trust You. Thank You for Your Spirit who indwells me. I pray that He will control me. Thank You for leading me onwards to that place You have prepared for me.

Personal Reflections

Bibliography

Bonar, Horatius, 'Thy way, not mine'.

Brother Lawrence, *The Practice of the Presence of God* (London & Oxford: Mowbray, new edition, 1977).

Browning, Elizabeth Barrett, 'Patience Taught by Nature', *The Oxford Book of Christian Verse* chosen and edited by Lord David Cecil (Oxford: Clarendon Press, 1940) 393.

Bunyan, John. 'Contentment', *Praying with the English Poets*, compiled and introduced by Ruth Etchells (London: SPCK, 1990) 31.

Bunyan, John, *He who would valiant be.*

Chichester, Richard of, *Day by Day.*

Conder, Josiah, *Day by day the manna fell* (*Sankey's Sacred Songs and Solos*)

Cowper, William, *Oh! for a closer walk with God.*

Crosby, Fanny J, *Blessed Assurance.*

Cushing, William O., *Down in the Valley.*

Havergal, Frances Ridley, *I am trusting Thee, Lord Jesus.*

Havergal, Frances Ridley, *Who is on the Lord's side?*

Herbert, George, 'The Call', *Praying with the English Poets*, compiled and introduced by Ruth Etchells (London: SPCK, 1990) 27

Hood, Edwin Paxton, *O walk with Jesus.*

Hopkins, Gerard Manley, 'Spring', *The Oxford book of Christian Verse*, chosen and edited by Lord David Cecil (Oxford: Clarendon Press, 1940) 496.

Jellie, W.H., *The Preacher's Homiletical Commentary on the Book of Jeremiah* (London: Ballantine Press, 1882).

Keats, John, 'What is more gentle than a wind in summer?', *Poetical Works*

(Oxford: Oxford University Press, 1956), 42.

Keats, John, 'Ode to Autumn', *Poetical Works* (Oxford: Oxford University Press, 1956) 218.

Kelly, Katherine Agnes May, *Give me a sight, O Saviour* (National Young Life Campaign).

Lavater, Johann Caspar, *O Jesus Christ, grow Thou in me*, translated by Elizabeth Lee Smith.

Lemmell, Helen H., *O soul, are you weary and troubled?* (Singspiration Music/Brentwood Benson Music Publishing, 1922).

Matheson, George, *O Light, that followest all my way.*

Newton, John, *Amazing Grace.*

Procter, Anne Adelaide, *My God, I thank Thee.*

Ramsey, Benjamin Mansell, *Teach me Thy way, O Lord.*

Robinson, George Wade, *Loved with Everlasting Love.*

Rossetti, Christina Georgina, 'In the Bleak Mid-Winter', *The Oxford Book of Christian Verse*, chosen and edited by Lord David Cecil (Oxford: Clarendon Press, 1940) 471.

Rossetti, Christina Georgina, 'If only…', *The Oxford Book of Christian Verse*, edited by Lord David Cecil (Oxford: Clarendon Press, 1940) 467.

Rother, Johann Andreas, *Father, Thine Everlasting Grace* (Translated by John Wesley).

Sammis, John Henry, *When we walk with the Lord.*

Scriven, Joseph, *What a friend we have in Jesus.*

Smote, Edward, *My hope is built on nothing less.*

Stewart, Alexander, *Jeremiah* (Edinburgh: Knox Press, 1936.)

St Francis of Assisi, 'Lord, make me an instrument of Thy peace'.

Thomson, James, 'A Hymn on the Seasons', *The Oxford Book of Christian Verse*, edited by Lord David Cecil (Oxford: Clarendon Press, 1940) 323.

Washbourne, Thomas, *Casting all your care upon God.*

Watts, Isaac, *Joy to the World.*

Wesley, Charles. *And can it be?*

Scripture Index

National Distributors

UK: (and countries not listed below)
CWR, Waverley Abbey House, Waverley Lane, Farnham, Surrey GU9 8EP.
Tel: (01252) 784700 Outside UK (+44) 1252 784700

AUSTRALIA: CMC Australasia, PO Box 519, Belmont, Victoria 3216.
Tel: (03) 5241 3288 Fax: (03) 5241 3290

CANADA: Cook Communications Ministries, PO Box 98, 55 Woodslee Avenue, Paris, Ontario N3L 3E5.
Tel: 1800 263 2664

GHANA: Challenge Enterprises of Ghana, PO Box 5723, Accra.
Tel: (021) 222437/223249 Fax: (021) 226227

HONG KONG: Cross Communications Ltd, 1/F, 562A Nathan Road, Kowloon.
Tel: 2780 1188 Fax: 2770 6229

INDIA: Crystal Communications, 10-3-18/4/1, East Marredpalli, Secunderabad – 500026, Andhra Pradesh.
Tel/Fax: (040) 27737145

KENYA: Keswick Books and Gifts Ltd, PO Box 10242, Nairobi.
Tel: (02) 331692/226047 Fax: (02) 728557

MALAYSIA: Salvation Book Centre (M) Sdn Bhd, 23 Jalan SS 2/64, 47300 Petaling Jaya, Selangor.
Tel: (03) 78766411/78766797 Fax: (03) 78757066/78756360

NEW ZEALAND: CMC Australasia, PO Box 36015, Lower Hutt.
Tel: 0800 449 408 Fax: 0800 449 049

NIGERIA: FBFM, Helen Baugh House, 96 St Finbarr's College Road, Akoka, Lagos.
Tel: (01) 7747429/4700218/825775/827264

PHILIPPINES: OMF Literature Inc, 776 Boni Avenue, Mandaluyong City.
Tel: (02) 531 2183 Fax: (02) 531 1960

SOUTH AFRICA: Struik Christian Books, 80 MacKenzie Street, PO Box 1144, Cape Town 8000.
Tel: (021) 462 4360 Fax: (021) 461 3612

SRI LANKA: Christombu Publications (Pvt) Ltd, Bartlett House, 65 Braybrooke Place, Colombo 2.
Tel: (9411) 2421073/2447665

TANZANIA: CLC Christian Book Centre, PO Box 1384, Mkwepu Street, Dar es Salaam.
Tel/Fax: (022) 2119439

USA: Cook Communications Ministries, PO Box 98, 55 Woodslee Avenue, Paris, Ontario N3L 3E5, Canada.
Tel: 1800 263 2664

ZIMBABWE: Word of Life Books (Pvt) Ltd, Christian Media Centre, 8 Aberdeen Road, Avondale,
PO Box A480 Avondale, Harare.
Tel: (04) 333355 or 091301188

For email addresses, visit the CWR website: www.cwr.org.uk
CWR is a registered charity – Number 294387
CWR is a limited company registered in England – Registration Number 1990308

Day and Residential Courses
Counselling Training
Leadership Development
Biblical Study Courses
Regional Seminars
Ministry to Women
Daily Devotionals
Books and Videos
Conference Centre

Trusted all Over the World

CWR HAS GAINED A WORLDWIDE reputation as a centre of excellence for Bible-based training and resources. From our headquarters at Waverley Abbey House, Farnham, England, we have been serving God's people for 40 years with a vision to help apply God's Word to everyday life and relationships. The daily devotional *Every Day with Jesus* is read by nearly a million readers an issue in more than 150 countries, and our unique courses in biblical studies and pastoral care are respected all over the world. Waverley Abbey House provides a conference centre in a tranquil setting.

For free brochures on our seminars and courses, conference facilities, or a catalogue of CWR resources, please contact us at the following address.
CWR, Waverley Abbey House, Waverley Lane, Farnham, Surrey GU9 8EP, UK

Telephone: **+44 (0)1252 784700**
Email: **mail@cwr.org.uk**
Website: **www.cwr.org.uk**

CWR Applying God's Word
to everyday life and relationships

Every Day with Jesus
Pocket Devotionals

The two latest volumes in the popular pocket devotional series, these are beautifully presented devotionals containing thoughts from the whole year by Selwyn Hughes. Designed to help you grow in your relationship with Jesus and enhance your spiritual journey, these pocket-sized books make ideal travelling companions or welcome gifts.

Walking in Faith
ISBN: 978-1-85345-399-1
£7.99 (plus p&p)

Joy for Today
ISBN: 978-1-85345-398-4
£7.99 (plus p&p)

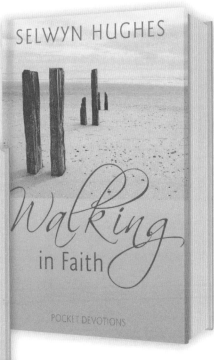